Mental WEALTH

Mental
WEALTH

A MANAGERS GUIDE TO
*Workplace Mental Health
and Wellbeing*

Emi Golding
and Peter Diaz

NEW YORK

LONDON • NASHVILLE • MELBOURNE • VANCOUVER

Mental WEALTH
A MANAGERS GUIDE TO
Workplace Mental Health and Wellbeing

Published in New York, New York, by Morgan James Publishing. Morgan James is a trademark of Morgan James, LLC. www.MorganJamesPublishing.com

The moral rights of the authors have been asserted

All inquiries should be made to the author.

Disclaimer
The material in this publication is of the nature of general comment only, and does not represent professional advice. It is not intended to provide specific guidance for particular circumstances and it should not be relied on as the basis for any decision to take action or not take action on any matter which it covers. Readers should obtain professional advice where appropriate, before making any such decision. To the maximum extent permitted by law, the author and publisher disclaim all responsibility and liability to any person, arising directly or indirectly from any person taking or not taking action based on the information in this publication.

ISBN 978-1-64279-366-6 paperback
ISBN 978-1-64279-367-3 eBook
Library of Congress Control Number: 2018913758

Cover Design by:
Rachel Lopez
www.r2cdesign.com

Interior Design by:
Bonnie Bushman
The Whole Caboodle Graphic Design

In an effort to support local communities, raise awareness and funds, Morgan James Publishing donates a percentage of all book sales for the life of each book to Habitat for Humanity Peninsula and Greater Williamsburg.

Get involved today! Visit
www.MorganJamesBuilds.com

Table of Contents

Preface   *vii*

Foreword   *x*

Introduction   *xiv*

PART ONE: THE PROBLEM WITH WORKPLACE   **1**
**   MENTAL HEALTH**

1. What is a Mental Illness?   3

2. Identifying Mental Health Issues   18

3. The Costs and Causes of Worsening Mental Health in
        the Workplace   44

4. The Manager's Role   64

PART TWO: THE 7 PILLARS OF A MENTALLY   **73**
**   WEALTHY WORKPLACE**

What is Mental Wealth?   75

Pillar 1: We Not You   78

Pillar 2: Organisational Plasticity   88

Pillar 3: Nothing About Me Without Me   98

Pillar 4: Total Integration   106

Pillar 5: Mutual Responsibility   111

Pillar 6: Understanding Complexity   117

Pillar 7: Wrap-around Strategies   123

Conclusion   129

About the Authors And the Workplace Mental Health Institute   *133*

Preface

Before you read further, there are some things you need to know.

1. This is a business book dealing with the sensitive topic of mental health at work. However, unlike other books you might read on the subject, it pulls no punches, because the most effective way to remove a Band-Aid is speedily and decisively.

    In a world where we are seeing increasing rates of mental health problems, increasing workplace stress, and increasing rates of suicide, this is vital. We need to make some changes and we need to make them yesterday.

2. At times, we use strong language to get across both the meaning and feeling of what we are trying to say. We hope you can forgive our language and understand that, working in the world of mental health, it is pretty common to come across some colourful turns of phrase. When people feel frustrated

and trapped, it's pretty normal for them to use strong language in an attempt to express the extent of their emotions. It's not personal.

3. This is neither a medical book nor a scientific treatise. Nor does it purport to be either. We will refer to so-and-so study here and there, and there are countless academic articles to back up what we will tell you. But this is not an academic thesis. We don't want to write one and we believe very few of you actually want to read one. If you are interested in exploring the science behind the concepts in this book, we will point you in the right direction, and we enthusiastically encourage you to do your own research.

4. This is not a book about therapy. And it's not a book to be used in a therapeutic setting. If you are suffering from a mental health problem, there are many other books that will be far more useful for you. We encourage you to pick up one of those instead. Having said that, as a manager or leader who wants to improve the mental health and wellbeing of your workforce, you might just find that some of the concepts within are also useful personally. In fact, that's what many people who attend our courses tell us all the time.

5. This book has been written specifically for managers. If you are a manager, or aspire to be one in the near future, then congratulations! What you are about to read will revolutionise the way you lead. If you aren't a manager… leave a copy somewhere for one to discover.

What we want for this book, and what we aspire to in our education programs, is to give managers the tools, skills and understanding to confidently and compassionately handle a range of mental health situations in the workplace. In the process, we help them become better communicators, with a more sophisticated understanding of workplace dynamics. By doing so, we hope to clear their path towards the success, enjoyment and fulfilment that comes with leading a high performance team.

Let's get started.

Yours in mental health,
Peter Diaz & Emi Golding
Directors
Workplace Mental Health Institute

Foreword

by Steve Anderson

Workplace mental health issues have been swept under the proverbial rug for too long.

As a business owner or manager, one of your responsibilities is to take care of your employees so they can take care of your customers. There is a lot of talk today about employee engagement and finding and retaining good employees in a challenging hiring environment. How your organization responds to mental health issues in your workplace affects your employees more than you know.

I have spent 40 years in the risk management and insurance business. I have seen firsthand the consequences of employee mental health problems: higher worker injury rates, decreased productivity, an increase in employment-related lawsuits, and in extreme cases, employee violence. Organizations of all types and sizes face real financial costs when they ignore this issue.

Of course, there are risks when you take action. When you do anything, there's a certain amount of risk involved. But I've also learned that if you don't act (hoping if you ignore the problem it will eventually go away), the risks that supervisors, managers, and the organization face could be even higher.

As a business or organization, are you at risk for a harassment or bullying claim being brought by the employee? *Mental Wealth* will help you understand how to manage that risk effectively.

Are you afraid of saying or doing the wrong thing? The *Mental Wealth* book will help you understand how to take the best approach for both your employee and your business.

Are you accountable for what you do (or don't do) regarding the mental health of your organization? *Mental Wealth* will help you look at both the physical as well as the fiscal responsibilities of creating a healthy organization and healthy, productive workers. It seems obvious, but prevention is more cost-effective than managing a crisis because when unaddressed, reaction to a problem after it's happened is the most expensive way for businesses to manage mental health.

Not taking proactive steps to address mental health issues that are in your workplace right now (and we all have them) could actually be the riskiest decision you make.

Too often, mental health issues are avoided because they are "messy" and best left to the professionals in Human Resources, Risk Management or the Health and Safety Department.

But in today's environment, everybody has to be on board.

That's why I was encouraged when I met Peter Diaz and Emi Golding some years ago when we were both part of a small intensive training group here in the US.

Over the days we were together, I listened to Peter and Emi describe the challenging issues of mental health in the workplace in Australia and their concern that mental health issues were not being proactively managed by many organizations. (The comparison to what is happening here in the US was strikingly familiar.)

Their passion for helping organizations address this issue head-on is impressive. They founded the Workplace Mental Health Institute to lead the fight to help individuals and organizations tackle this complex problem with proven, effective plans and strategies.

I have watched as both Peter and Emi traveled the world the last few years providing workshops and seminars for Fortune 500 companies, large and medium organizations, and government departments. They have trained thousands of managers and supervisors on the importance of taking care of employees' well-being and how to tackle the mental health epidemic in the most effective way.

I don't know of a better team than Peter and Emi. Their energy, education, and passion for helping businesses of all sizes improve the workplace and well-being environment are exceptional. *Mental Wealth* provides you with access to their vast knowledge and experience in a practical and useful format.

Peter and Emi have identified Seven Pillars you can use to build a mentally wealthy workplace. You will find this section to be your "plan of action" for what to do next. For each of the pillars, they provide a section on "How do you apply this pillar?" as well as specific initiatives you can take within your organization immediately to implement a safer and more responsive workplace.

Both Peter and Emi have the knowledge, skills, credentials, and experience to guide you through this process. Peter is also upfront about his personal encounters with mental health issues, providing sage insight and perspective. Their credentials are extensive, but more importantly, they have real-life experience working with organizations worldwide. They don't just bring an academic view; their decades of experience have helped them to address practical problems, (expected) resistance, and the unique challenges organizations face.

Mental Wealth is a very appropriate title for this book. As they described in their introduction, this is not a textbook or academic paper. It is your guide for what to do, when to do it, and how to do it.

Remember what I said about higher worker injury rates, decreased productivity, an increase in employment-related lawsuits, and in extreme cases, employee violence? Again, organizations of all types and sizes face real financial costs when they ignore this issue.

That's why this book is so important. It helps you understand the issues and provides you with practical language, steps, and processes you can take to effectively create a Mentally Wealthy workplace.

Your organization *will* address mental health issues in the workplace at some point in the future. Creating *Mental Wealth* is an excellent first step to begin the process of enhancing your workplace culture to better care for employees so they can better care for your customers.

Steve Anderson

LinkedIn Influencer and a trusted authority on Insurance Technology, Productivity and Innovation. He has over 35 years of experience in the insurance community and holds a master's degree in Insurance Law.

Introduction

There's a scene in the movie *Zulu Dawn* where the British are facing down a charge of thousands of Zulu warriors. Desperate to halt the decimation of his company at the hands of the Zulus, a British sergeant pleads for the third time with the Quartermaster for more ammunition. The officer, a stickler for procedure, tells the sergeant to wait his turn at the back of the line. Off to the side, another officer is sitting down calmly sipping his tea or some other thing. Unlike the sergeant, both officers are oblivious to the carnage unfolding.

This scene makes me think of the current state of mental health in the workplace. There's carnage unfolding, but many leaders seem either oblivious to it or overly focused on following proper procedure—whatever that is.

Each year, one in four people suffer from a mental disorder. The suicide rate has gone up over the past few years, to the point at which, around the world, someone takes their own life every forty seconds. In

Western countries, like Canada, Australia, the United States and the United Kingdom, the average psychological injury claim now costs $250,000 and the number of claims is rising. It's clear that whatever we've been doing to address this issue is not working.

As a business leader, in whatever capacity, whether you're a manager, supervisor, team leader or CEO, it's time to do something about it.

The manager both willing and able to act in these urgent times stands to gain a significant competitive advantage. There's a direct and powerful link between a team's mental health and the quality and quantity of output for a business. We like to call it Mental Wealth.

....

Mental Wealth—the link between a team's mental health and the bottom line

....

A manager with the ability to join the dots and see how taking care of his or her team's mental health impacts the bottom line is rare.

So we take this opportunity to congratulate you for taking the time to read this book. What you learn from this book will equip you to build a happy, resilient, high-performing team. In doing so, you will be helping to address the mental health epidemic we see globally.

As mental health experts who have worked with hundreds of organisations, from small businesses through to multinational corporations, we've seen just how powerful it can be for the businesses, and the people in them, when workplaces are transformed into happy, healthy and psychologically safe places to be.

Why aren't we doing more?

How can it be that one in four adults suffer from a mental disorder each year? And given how clearly mental health problems are impacting organisations and the people in them, why isn't more being done about it? To understand why, we need to look at the dynamics between the players in our organisations and ask ourselves what might be stopping them from taking action.

Why aren't organisations doing more?

We've consulted with and delivered training to thousands of leaders from a range of industries, including finance, law, defence, mining, education, health, hospitality, and many more. This experience has put us in a unique and trusted position to identify some of the key challenges organisations face in regard to addressing workplace mental health issues.

It's not on the radar

For some organisations, the reason they aren't doing more is that they have simply never considered this to be an area they should be thinking about in the workplace. It is happening less often now, but from time to time, our office will receive a call from a Human Resource Director who is looking for help because there has been a serious mental health incident in the workplace, and they have just realised that workplace mental health is a 'thing' they should be paying attention to. Especially in the case of suicide, it's a matter of too little, too late. In these cases, there is a lot of work to be done to support the staff (and the managers) who have just lost a colleague. It also means that when it comes to delivering subsequent mental health education, the loss of the team members' colleague and friend will be forefront in their mind and influence the way the mental health education is received. I'm sure I don't have to tell you that it would have been much better to provide this guidance *BEFORE* a crisis happened, not after.

Not prioritising the issue

Then there are those organisations who know it is something that really needs to be addressed; they are even aware it is having an impact on their teams. The problem is they have other competing demands, and without there having been an overt crisis situation, they don't see an immediate need to take action in this area. They'll say, 'Well, it's on the agenda, but we have to wait until after the restructure / certain job roles are filled / another project is finished.' In these cases, we can't stress enough the importance of prioritising this issue. Not only could pushing it to one side cost lives, it is already costing the business thousands of dollars in lost productivity through absenteeism, presenteeism and conflict.

Narrow focus on motivation and competence

Most organisations fail to grasp that many chronic Human Resource (HR) issues are, in fact, the result of mental health issues. Isolated, individual mistakes or failures are unlikely to result in performance management action. By the time an issue comes across the desk of a senior manager or HR manager, it's likely to be a pattern of conflict or behaviour that hasn't been resolved by the parties involved. The traditional performance management model focuses on complying with behavioural standards and meeting a remedial plan of action; it rarely gets into the underlying issues driving the problem behaviour. However, these are exactly what need to be addressed in order to produce a sustainable solution.

An attitude that people are replaceable

Compassion is often the first value to be sacrificed on the altar of financial performance. Highly competitive cultures expect (and, indeed, build into their recruiting models) an allowance for employee attrition. They figure they can run the organisation at such a pace as to 'shake loose' an acceptable percentage of their workforce (the weaker ones) and replace them with fresh recruits. What these companies don't understand is the hidden cost of attrition, often estimated at 100 per cent of the annual salary of each person who leaves. There is certainly a financial case (notwithstanding the moral one) for building organisational resilience and maximising retention.

Willingness to make excuses

In any given organisation, there are some people who are just toxic. Everyone knows who they are, from the most junior employee to the CEO. And, yet, they're allowed to remain. Maybe they're the top salesperson, bringing in ten times their salary every quarter. Maybe they're the IT guy, who's the only one who knows how the system works. They are so important in the short to medium term that it's worth putting up with their behaviour. But herein lies a slow killer: In time, your organisation will be stuck with B players, because your talent (with other options) will leave. Your managers will be less effective when it comes to managing performance because of the glaring double standard. And, in time, the culture will be so entrenched, the cancer so advanced, that change would need to be so broad and intense that the treatment might risk killing the host.

The reality is that all the players in the organisation must work together to address mental health. The risks of getting it wrong are manageable, given the right training and a genuine desire to make a change for the better. So why is it, at the moment, that the different players aren't doing more to address the issue?

Why aren't managers doing more?

The prevailing management style through much of the last couple of centuries has been to keep a professional distance from staff members. The manager's job was to set the direction and manage the performance of the employee, and the employee's job was to reliably perform their tasks to the best of their ability. It's a similar relationship to that between a machine and its operator, which is not surprising, given much of the industrialisation-era work was done by men in factories. Employees were cogs in a machine, so to speak, and much of the management and HR thinking was (and still is) centred around ensuring enough employees were available to maintain production, and that they performed reliably and at maximum efficiency. It would be ridiculous for an operator to ask his machine, 'Are you okay?' Similarly, many managers today feel that asking an employee about their mental state is not appropriate—it's too personal. It's taboo. It seems the prevailing management paradigm is fundamentally not equipped to deal with mental health issues.

Here are some of the concerns that stop managers from stepping up and doing more:

Will this look like harassment?

For managers who do decide to wade into a mental health issue, a real concern is how the employee will react. What if the employee takes exception to the line of questioning? What if they feel so put out that they lodge a formal complaint against the manager for harassment? This is a valid concern, as they're likely to be dealing with a person in a heightened state of sensitivity, with many people with a mental health issue reporting that they feel bullied or harassed more often. For a manager, having a workplace harassment or bullying judgement go against them has serious consequences: The organisation may be liable for damages, and the manager themselves may be personally liable. This can seriously curtail that manager's confidence and ability to manage performance thereafter. Once bitten, twice shy.

What if I make it worse?

In reality (and we'll discuss this later), the risk of a successful harassment or bullying claim being brought against a manager for addressing a mental health concern is very low, when done properly. And therein lies the challenge: 'properly'. Many managers who are genuinely concerned about an employee's mental health will avoid addressing it for fear of doing something that makes things worse. 'What if I say the wrong thing?' 'What if I embarrass them?' 'Should I just report it to someone?' These are all common questions that go through a manager's head. These are valid questions, by the way— managing a mental health issue in a team does take a set of skills. The reason most managers don't feel confident with this stuff is that they've never been taught the skills. In no business degree or MBA or even HR qualification that we know of are mental health management skills taught. We ask in every one of our courses and, to date, we have not had any HR professional EVER indicate that they were trained in managing mental health as part of their studies. Managers are really left to rely on their own experience and their emotional intelligence to deal with these situations. And in allowing that to happen, frankly, we are letting our managers down.

I really don't have time for this

We don't have to look far to realise that managers across the country are overworked. I don't mean in a 'we just say we're busy so people think we're useful' kind of way—I mean many of our organisations are chronically under-resourced. The downsizing and delayering of middle management in the late eighties and early nineties was taken too far. To use a medical analogy, companies went beyond 'cutting out the fat' and have cut out some of the minor muscle groups. Line and middle managers in particular are seeing their workloads and responsibilities grow for little to no extra resources or compensation as organisations downsize and rationalise. Many managers simply do not have the headspace or the energy to involve themselves in the mental health of their employees—they're flat out managing their own.

Why aren't individuals doing more?

Looking at the reasons organisations and managers aren't doing more begs the question why the individuals suffering don't do more to draw attention to the issues they are facing. One thing people often don't consider is that individuals don't realise to what extent their mental health is suffering. Another consideration is the stigma such issues are still subject to, especially in some workplace cultures. These are some of the attitudes that stop individuals from seeking help themselves:

It's just stress

The most common mental illnesses (anxiety and depression) tend to be insidious, in that they gradually worsen over time. Many sufferers don't even realise they have a mental health issue until it's been months or even years since they've felt happy and their situation is quite progressed. It's convenient for a sufferer to dismiss their experience as temporary or 'just stress'. But there is a difference between 'stress' and something more serious.

I should just suck it up

People tend to compare themselves to others, and if everyone else seems fine, then they don't want to be the exception, or the 'weak one'. People will compare themselves to their parents who did it tough and never complained. The truth is that it's likely they faced the same issues and felt the same way; it's just that the conditions were less understood and there weren't the resources widely available to assist them. It's also very easy to feel inadequate when you're seeing all your friends on social media having a great time and appearing successful, when the reality is that, while few people share their fears and failures for all to see, they most certainly have issues you're unaware of. When everyone around you seems to be coping and thriving, the act of admitting you need help and seeking it out can make you feel like you've failed somehow.

And a lot of people would rather endure the symptoms than admit they need help.

Bringing this up would be career suicide

Numerous surveys from Australia, the UK, the US and Canada have shown that people with a mental illness are unlikely to disclose it to their employer for fear of being treated less favourably. Even employment lawyers have been heard advising employees to think twice before disclosing their mental health problem. Many employees believe that, if they disclose, they'll be passed over for project and promotion opportunities, or that their reputation or 'internal brand' will be tarnished, or that the organisation will take steps to exit them.

Why aren't colleagues doing more?

So the above takes into account why organisations, management and individuals themselves aren't doing more to work on mental health issues in the workplace, but what about a sufferer's teammates? There are yet more considerations that stop a person's colleagues from taking action in this area. Here are some of the attitudes that challenge them:

If you can't cut it, you shouldn't be here

In highly competitive teams, being able to tolerate the stresses and challenges of a role or industry and win consistently forms part of the team's identity, and underpins the self-esteem of individual members. If a team member is struggling to cope, then surely that says something about that person's fit? It's this zero sum mentality that says, 'Well, if that guy gets special treatment, it's going to be more work for me.' What's interesting is how many team members in these 'dog eat dog' cultures are themselves on the verge of burnout. The person who puts their hand up and asks for help is the classic canary in the coal mine.

I don't want to overstep the bounds

In some teams, having a team member ask another member about their mental health would strengthen the bonds within the team and lead to higher performance. In other teams, it would lead to an erosion of performance. The difference? Trust. In teams that lack trust, a member asking such a question could be construed as their having a hidden agenda. It also raises the question for the individual: 'If they're flat out asking me to my face, what have they been saying behind my back?' This doubt about how a colleague's actions will be perceived can block dialogue before it even happens.

I might make things worse

Team members share this common concern with managers. Both are worried that their well-intentioned efforts to address a team member's mental health could have unintended consequences. No one wants to have on their conscience the idea that their actions tipped a person over the edge, and so they think it's safer to ignore an issue and hope it works itself out soon. Again, it's lack of training and actionable skills that are missing. Traditional mental health awareness training and promotion calls on people to ask, 'Are you okay?' but fails to suggest what to do if the answer is 'No.'

Deciding to do nothing has resulted in a conspiracy of silence in our organisations. It has created environments where many people know about an individual's mental health challenges, but no one raises it with them. It's only a matter of time before the individual finds out that people are discussing them behind their back, if they're aren't already aware. This erodes trust, which is the key element in a high-performing team. I hope it's as obvious to you as it is to me that, if we're to have high-performing teams, something has to change in our approach.

What's the business case for addressing mental health?

It's obvious that mental health disorders have an enormous impact on the quality of life of many employees. But let's for a minute set aside the social and moral case for change, and focus solely on the bottom line.

It can be difficult to quantify the financial benefits of investing in mental health, because the link between mental health and money is not a direct one. However, there have been some attempts in recent years to talk about mental health in terms of the dollars.

A 2014 study by consultants Price Waterhouse Coopers (PwC) found that businesses could see an average return of $2.30 for every $1 invested in improving employee mental health. In some industries, it was even higher—up to $11 for every $1 invested.

> **'Importantly, the results of this analysis are conservative as they do not consider the full range of costs to an organisation caused by untreated mental health conditions, such as high turnover. Estimates also do not include the many intangible benefits of a mentally healthy workplace for all employees, such as improved morale. This potential for additional benefits further reinforces the business case to invest in mental health.' –PwC**

When it comes to investing in mental health, what the executive team needs to realise is that, as opposed to seeing an increase in revenue (although that can happen when the workforce is happy, healthy and feeling motivated to produce), they are most likely to see this return in terms of costs saved—from absenteeism, presenteeism, psychological and physical injury claims, and reduced turnover, etc. These are areas where mental illness is *already costing* the business.

They may not be glaringly obvious in a profit and loss statement, because they're not listed under 'mental health', but they are most definitely there.

What PwC was able to quantify is something we know intuitively to be true: Poor mental health costs businesses money, and good mental health increases profitability.

The legal rationale

For employers not too concerned with the financial impact of mental health, there are legal considerations to take into account. They differ slightly from country to country, but among Western countries, there are the same basic concepts:

- Workplace Health & Safety legislation states that employers must provide a safe and healthy workplace that does not cause physical or mental ill health or aggravate existing conditions.
- Disability Discrimination legislation says that employers must not discriminate or harass employees with mental health conditions. That includes taking no adverse action against an employee because of a mental health condition.
- Privacy legislation requires that employees' personal information (such as about their health) should be kept private.

The challenge with legislation like this is that, while it's great to hold workplaces responsible for ensuring a psychologically safe working environment, it doesn't say what workplaces are actually required to do. What constitutes a psychologically safe workplace? What does it look like? And what activities are considered reasonable for a workplace to implement? Here, employers are left in the dark. And given that this is a pretty new area to be included in legislation, there don't really exist many precedents to base our answers to these questions on. Workplace mental health can be a bit of a legal quagmire, but it is an issue you can't avoid.

What about the people?

Besides the financial and legal rationale for addressing workplace mental health, there are, of course, the people involved. People are the lifeblood of an organisation. No matter how many machines or automations you build into your business, at the end of the day, there will always be a certain number of people required to operate them, to think creatively about business solutions for the future, and to solve problems when they arise.

Culture

When mental health issues impact the workplace, everyone is affected. If the person remains in the workplace, their energy can influence the rest of the team, and can be a drain on the unprepared manager. Before you know it, there is conflict, poor morale and negativity. If they are absent, it is often for an unknown period of time, during which the other team members have to pick up the slack, doing extra work for no extra benefit. Resentment can build, people can start to slack off, and the manager then needs to address further issues. Sometimes, they don't. Regardless, the culture and morale head south.

Creativity

Another concern is this intangible thing called 'creativity'. When an organisational culture becomes highly stressed, perhaps even toxic, I guarantee you that the first virtue to go will be creativity. Why? It's in the way our brains are wired. Our abilities to be creative and to cooperate socially have evolved over time as our brains have evolved.

A long way back on our evolutionary journey, our brain was concerned only with survival and mating. When we were threatened, our amygdala would react immediately to get us out of trouble. Our heart would beat faster to fuel our muscles with more oxygen to fight or flee and our attention would narrow to the immediate task at hand. Later, our 'mammalian' brain evolved and that allowed us to live in groups and cooperate to share resources and improve our odds of survival. And, finally, our frontal lobes and prefrontal lobes evolved to put us over the top in terms of intelligence and creative problem solving.

When a cave bear has spotted you and is making its way over, you don't want to concern yourself with whether the bear's just had a bad day, or if it's his way of relating to you. Likewise, you don't have time to construct an ingenious escape strategy involving a garbage bag, four zip ties and a washing machine motor. No, you just need to run (faster than one other person in your group).

What happens in a workplace setting when confronted with a threat such as perceived lack of resources (e.g. deadline pressure), attack from a rival (e.g. competition for a promotion), or expulsion from the group (e.g. screwing up a project) is that the primitive brain takes over and we act in the crazy ways people act that make us wonder, 'What's gotten into that guy?'

You can see that, for organisations with a win-at-all-costs, dog-eat-dog culture, it's physiologically improbable that they will be creative, innovative companies that people are drawn to. And that's what our companies need to be these days in order for the people to thrive.

Recruitment & Reputation

More and more, these days, people are not necessarily looking for the highest paying job. They are looking for work which is fulfilling, which fits into their lifestyle, and which they enjoy going to. Creating a mentally healthy and positive workplace environment leads to a workforce of people who are happy and productive, and who become ambassadors for your brand. As you become known as an employer of choice, you will be able to attract and retain greater talent.

Community

It would be naïve to think that people always leave work at work. Instead, people take these stresses home to their families. They are irritable about something that happened at work and end up having a fight with their spouse. They are exhausted and have no energy for playing with the kids. They start drinking or eating after work each day to 'recover' from the tense work environment. And this then creates a negative cycle when they go back into the workplace. People are people wherever they are.

If not for financial and legal reasons, we should be addressing workplace mental health because it is the right thing to do for our communities.

It Could be You

One overriding fact to take into account is that mental health disorders do not discriminate, so neither should we.

Some people think that if you have a mental health disorder, you must be weak or deficient in some way. The truth is, mental health disorders don't discriminate—they are just as likely to affect your best and brightest talents, your solid industry stalwarts and your high flying CEOs as they are to afflict your more sensitive, introverted employee stereotypes.

What About the Future?

We really are at a critical time in our history of work. For centuries, we have used a model of work from the industrial revolution, but the time has come when that is no longer serving us. People are not machines, and they will not stand for being treated like machines anymore. We are diverse, and we demand that our diversity be respected and recognised.

We want freedom, we want to be heard, and we want to have choices. As evidence, just look to the growing numbers of people turning to freelancing and solo-preneurship as a way of supporting their lifestyle.

Workplaces are changing too. With increasing economic uncertainty, businesses are being forced to do more with less. We are downsizing, restructuring and reshaping the way we do work. Add in technology, where we are looking at a very near future with even more use of robots, automation and virtual reality in the workplace. We have globalisation, where someone on the other side of the world can do the same job, or better, for a fraction of the cost. And all these changes are happening at an ever-increasing pace, causing fear and uncertainty for many.

Clearly, the way we work needs to change, and it needs to become more human. We need to support the mental health and wellbeing of our workforces and our communities in order to thrive.

Why are Managers the Key?

Why a book for managers? Because you, the manager, are pivotal to your team's mental health. No, that doesn't mean it's your 'fault' if someone in your team doesn't feel well. But it does mean that your people watch you like a hawk. They are watching how you do things, what you talk about, even what expressions you use. They're drawing conclusions about your behaviour in order to decide how they should act. This is so even if they hate your guts, because you are still the nominated leader. Research has shown time and again that people leave bosses, not jobs. That means you are massively influential—for better or worse.

Now, let's be honest. If you're like most managers, even HR specialists, you don't really know the first thing about managing mental health. And why on earth would you? It's not something you learn in management school, is it? Yet, as a manager, you're on the front line when it comes to dealing with the mental health of team members. You do the best you can. But the truth is, it's bloody hard, as well as annoying, to have to stop everything and give your undivided attention to these matters. It's also scary: What if you screw it up?

When we first started delivering mental health education over a decade ago, we found that many organisations wanting to address the mental health and wellbeing of their staff would get a group of people together and send them along to one of our public courses, or organize an in-house course, and send all their frontline people. That was great! It was fantastic to introduce these exciting concepts to employees, and teach them how to look after themselves and each other. But one thing we kept hearing again and again from participants was: 'This is great stuff—if only my manager was here,' or 'I'd love to implement this at work, but I don't have the authority.' Not only that, but we had a hunch that genuine workplace mental health and wellbeing relied upon something more than a bit of 'awareness training' and good intentions.

Mental health and wellbeing is impacted by so many areas of the workplace, including policies, systems and cultural aspects.

Mental health in organisations is impacted by both factors of content and context. This means that an individual's resilience is very important but so are the environment, culture and systems the individual is in. Hence, the saying: 'Before you decide you are depressed, make sure you are not just surrounded by a**holes.'

Think about this for a minute. Who has the most influence over these areas? Whom do people spend more time with during the day than their own family and friends? That's right—their managers. We believe you, as a manager, are best placed to spot the warning signs of mental distress and take action before things get out of control. And if you're to be responsible for getting the best out of your team in a high-pressure environment, why shouldn't you be given the tools to build and maintain resilience? Quick-fix Band-Aid solutions won't do.

Managing mental health is not about palming a person off to an Employee Assistance Program for a couple of sessions. It's not about sending them home on sick leave until they're better. It's about keeping an eye out for certain behaviours and applying some practical strategies to facilitate the recovery of a team member back to high performance.

So, have I got your attention? It's simple: Bad mental health is VERY bad for you and your business, costing the economy billions of dollars every year. Good mental health is fun and means lots of good returns for you and your business. While poor managerial practices equal bad mental health, managers with good mental-health practices have extraordinary teams.

Building a Commando Team

Whether it's through education on one of our courses, or consulting with the senior leaders of an organisation, what we try to help managers build is symbolized in the metaphor of the **commando team**. The commando team is a high-performing team. You can drop them in the middle of nowhere and they will do whatever they can to succeed in their mission. They are highly skilled and expertly trained and they have the mental stamina to get the job done. They don't stop because someone has a paper cut or a cold. And because they have a sense of purpose and know clearly what the mission is, they are highly valuable to whoever employs them.

The members of the commando team have each other's backs. There is a strong sense of camaraderie. The stakes are high and there is plenty of pressure. It is even possible in this mission that someone could get shot—but it won't be because they let each other down. Team members are in it together. Relationships with strong bonds are formed, and the team is not only high performing, but powerful.

This is what is available to every single manager—the opportunity to become the type of leader who is in charge of high-performing teams that operate in this powerful way.

Such leaders minimise mental health issues for their team. They pick up on the energy of the team fairly early on, and they know what will help protect their team and prevent stress, even within pressure-filled situations. Though no one can completely get rid of mental health problems, at least when someone does have an issue, the team is equipped to enable that person to continue working alongside them, operating to high capacity as much as possible. The leader creates an environment that is rich in recovery opportunities because of the way the team behaves.

This is the difference between a manager and a leader. Manager is a job title—a position in the hierarchy. A leader is the person who guides, influences and motivates others. To succeed in workplace mental health, you must take up the challenge to become a leader.

Improving mental health in the workplace

The aim of this book is to help you become a leader who can positively influence the way mental health is addressed in your organisation. It achieves this in two parts:

Part One: The problem with workplace mental health

The first part of the book exists to help you to understand just what we mean when we talk about mental health, why it is an issue in the workplace, whether it is getting worse, how it is that this issue isn't being addressed (or is being addressed in the wrong ways), and what you, as a manager, have to do with the problem.

Part Two: The 7 pillars of a mentally wealthy workplace

The second part of the book turns to the solution—fostering mental wealth. We have developed seven pillars which we consider to be the foundation of a mentally wealthy workplace. In this part of the book, we look at the elements that feed into each pillar and offer practical guidance to help you establish these pillars in your own organisation.

Our philosophy is simple. If it's good for your people, it's good for your pocket. And if you're not getting results, then it isn't working! In fact, we've seen a lot of 'wellbeing programs' do more harm than good, because managers were misinformed about what was really needed. When it comes to mental health, the stakes can be very high. This is not something you want to get wrong.

Workplace mental health is a complex matter. It's not necessarily easy to address, but there are some simple things which can make a huge difference. Other things seem simple yet take a lot of perseverance to implement. The people who think workplace mental health is a 'soft' topic gravely misunderstand the matter. There is nothing 'soft' about mental health. The reality is, to properly address workplace mental health, you have to be a strong leader or willing to become one. Our guess is you are that leader. So, buckle up and enjoy the ride. You'll get a lot out of this; we guarantee it.

PART ONE

The Problem With Workplace Mental Health

1

What is a Mental Illness?

O ne of the questions we like to open our workshops with is: 'How would you define a mental illness?' We're always surprised by the diversity of answers and the perspectives taken. Some people describe it from the perspective of the person with the condition; others describe it from an observer's viewpoint; still others from the person on the 'receiving end'.

These are some of the more popular themes:

- Behaviour that is irrational or risky
- An unstable emotional state
- Negative thoughts
- A chemical imbalance in the brain
- A genetic condition

- Dysfunctional relationships
- An illness or a disease
- Something that impacts on work and life
- Feeling sad, anxious, lost, overwhelmed or misunderstood
- Causes disability
- Disconnection from anything that matters
- A condition that requires a diagnosis from a professional, such as a GP or a psychologist

The first thing that stands out to us about these ideas is just how many of them fail to actually define something. They are saying it is 'something that' affects mood, 'something that' affects behaviours', 'something that' causes disability. Yet we really struggle to determine what the 'something' is.

Looking at these themes, the last definition, 'a condition that requires diagnosis from a professional', is usually offered by an educated and thoughtful audience member. It's my favourite, though, because it comes with one h*** of a kicker:

There is actually no consensus among experts on what mental disorder is.

A number of very clever people have published a bunch of very impressive papers, but at the end of the day, there is no actual consensus amongst professionals. There is one giant publication, *The Diagnostic & Statistical Manual of Mental Disorders* (DSM), which was put together by the American Psychiatric Association and presents a list of every diagnosis that one could be given. However, not everyone agrees with what is written in it. One of the biggest bones of contention is the fact that we are up to version five of this manual. Now, reviews and revisions are not a bad thing, generally, but in this case, there are some very telling problems.

What's wrong with the DSM?

Firstly, if we look to previous versions of this manual, in the original 1952 version, there were 106 different mental health diagnoses that one could be given. In the latest version, we have 297. Is it really possible that society has suddenly developed so many more types of mental health problems, which previously never existed, or is one of the following options more likely?

- That our current society has a tendency to over-medicalise what once used to be considered normal emotions and experiences.
- That the creators of this manual have a personal interest in the creation of more problems (as they can offer solutions). It's noteworthy that, at the last count, over sixty nine per cent of the panellists for the DSM 5 acknowledged taking large bonuses from various pharmaceutical companies.

There's more. Not only has the number of potential diagnoses grown, but the criteria for diagnosis has also changed substantially in relation to severity, duration and symptoms experienced. For example, one of the hotly debated areas in the current version is grief. Previous versions directed that if a person had experienced bereavement, they could not be diagnosed with depression for at least two months. (Interestingly, other forms of loss like loss of job, marriage, finances, etc., were not granted the same exemption.) However, the exemption for bereavement has now been removed, meaning that if a person grieves for more than two weeks, they can be diagnosed with depression. It follows that medication can then be prescribed. However, many would disagree with feelings of grief being defined as depression so quickly. There are some technical details about this that I won't go into here, but the fact remains that these criteria are not based on scientific test or study, but on the consensus of the current group of psychiatrists involved in the publication.

Furthermore, the fact that certain diagnoses have been added and removed makes the underlying scientific basis for their inclusion highly questionable. For example, in early versions of the manual, it was considered a mental disorder if someone believed in God. This was removed in later versions of the manual. Similarly, homosexuality was considered a mental disorder for many years, and many people were subjected to painful and humiliating 'shock treatment' in an attempt to cure them of the mental disorder. This was removed from the DSM as an official disorder in 1974, yet replaced with 'sexual orientation disturbance' which has a more vague definition. It makes one wonder what diagnoses in the current version will later be discredited as society becomes more accepting and tolerant of difference and emotional experience.

It is telling that when the current version of the DSM was being written, a number of petitions and critical responses were submitted from bodies such as the American Psychological Association, the British Psychological Association and the American Counselling Association, in an attempt to address a plethora of problematic diagnoses and criteria. However, it was to little effect.

If you want even more supporting evidence, then look at the book itself. It is called *The Diagnostic and Statistical Manual of **Mental Disorders***. Not *Mental Illness*. Even the most medical of medical professions stops short of actually calling such issues illness.

The DSM itself notes that: 'No definition adequately specifies precise boundaries for the concept of 'mental disorder'… different situations call for different definition.' It further states: 'There is no assumption that each category of mental disorder is a completely discrete entity with absolute boundaries dividing it from other mental disorders or from no mental disorder.'

If our most recognised source of mental health information is actually a book of unproven theories, which keeps changing with the flavour of the day, we really are stuck between a rock and a hard place.

And if we don't really know what a 'mental illness' is, then why is the term 'mental illness' so prevalent? For this, we need to look to history.

Why is the term 'mental illness' so common?

Think back to the old movies you've seen, from around, say, the 19th century. When you take a look at the street scenes of commoners going about their daily work, there is inevitably some poor crazy man or woman, dirty from the street, cast out and rejected by society. To be considered crazy was to be disowned, and people in mental or emotional distress were discarded to fend for themselves. It wasn't that long ago that this treatment was usual. Unfortunately, in some situations, it is still in evidence.

Enter the medical profession in the early 1900s. Remember, doctors were previously referred to as 'quacks', but they now started to gain status. They were good people who cared for those suffering with mental health problems, or maybe just wanted to get them off the streets. Either way, they decided to set up big institutions—the early psychiatric hospitals. These provided mentally unwell people with food, shelter and relative safety. The view was that these problems were permanent, so it was expected that people would live the rest of their life there, being 'treated' by doctors (though with no expectation of recovery).

Along with these developments came a shift in the way we thought about mental health. In order to reduce the stigma surrounding such issues, the medical establishment started to refer to mental distress as mental 'illness'. It helped the general population to compare it to physical problems, and shift the blame away from the person themselves and onto the 'illness'.

This kind of thinking still exists today. And, no doubt, for some, it is very helpful to think of mental distress as an 'illness'. It does reduce stigma, and it does mean that some people who would otherwise be less likely to get help are more willing to seek it. However, there has not, to date, been proof of any underlying disease or biological illness, so to speak. There is a feeling of being unwell, or ill, but no proven physical condition—that would be impossible, given that it is a 'mental' illness, hence, of the mind, not the physical body. Given this, the term mental illness is actually an oxymoron.

> To learn more, check out *The Myth of Mental Illness, "*
> written by eminent psychiatrist Dr Thomas Szasz.

The theory of chemical imbalance

A popular medical explanation blames mental distress on chemical imbalance. But, again, this is actually yet to be proven—it is still a theory (albeit one widely promoted by the pharmaceutical industry).

Now, before you dismiss us as whacko conspiracy theorists, listen to the facts and make your own judgements. When someone begins to feel unwell, mentally or emotionally, their first stop is usually their GP. For physical conditions, there is often some test which can be done to confirm a diagnosis—whether it is a blood test, a biopsy, an x-ray or some other scan. And that's a good idea—you want to get a thorough physical check. But if physical causes are ruled out and symptoms persist, people are likely to be told that their condition is down to a chemical imbalance in the brain. There's no test that confirms this—no analysis, nothing. Regardless, on this basis, people are prescribed medications to address the purported imbalance.

For argument's sake, let's suppose the cause of mental distress *is* a chemical imbalance in the brain.

Consider this: We know that the brain creates and regulates our thoughts and emotions. It follows that every emotion we experience could be considered a chemical imbalance in the brain—whether positive or negative, mild or strong. When you are happy, or excited, you are having a chemical imbalance in the brain. When you are worried or sad, there is a chemical imbalance in the brain. We all experience emotions, and chemical imbalances, all the time. So on the basis of someone experiencing certain emotions, to say they have a chemical imbalance in the brain is really stating the obvious.

What's difficult to ascertain is whether the chemical imbalance causes the emotion, or whether something, either in the external world or in our inner world of thought and emotion, has led to the chemical response. Chicken or egg? For example, we recently came across a course participant who shared during the break that they had recently separated from their spouse. This had meant selling the family home, splitting their assets, and beginning a whole new life at the age of sixty. They were experiencing the signs and symptoms of depression. Now, would you expect the cause of such depression to be 'a chemical imbalance in the brain'? Or perhaps a natural human reaction to the current situation?

Of course, the pain, suffering and distress still exist. We don't want to minimise that. But the course of treatment will depend on what you perceive to be the cause of the problems.

If it is something 'external', then the best approach to treating mental distress would be to consider the cause of the emotions rather than the subsequent chemical response. You would likely prescribe that the person seek some counselling or psychotherapy, support from friends and other services, and do things that will help them get through this difficult time.

Meanwhile, if you believe that chemical imbalance leads to the subsequent emotions, do you really think we should be adding more chemicals to the mix? Many people, including some from practicing medical establishments, would agree that medication ought to be the last alternative. Unfortunately, what we see is doctors using drugs as their primary response. This can be dangerous. In fact, an experienced psychiatrist, Dr Peter Breggin, argues that attempting to treat psychological conditions by artificially introducing chemicals can reduce the ability of the brain to create its own chemicals in the future. This creates a state of dependence on medications. And we do, in fact, see the signs of addiction just as we do with any other drug—physical dependence, psychological dependence, and withdrawal when people attempt to stop taking medication. Doctors will tell you never to stop such medication abruptly, and without the support of your physician, as it can be dangerous to your health. These are serious drugs we are talking about here! Not something to be taken lightly, or prescribed so easily. And we haven't even begun to speak about the known side effects!

Now, we didn't intend to get into a rant about medications, but these are things that managers need to have an understanding of if they are going to really grasp the complexity of mental health issues in the workplace.

We need to make it very clear here—we are not against the use of psychiatric medications, when used responsibly, in appropriate dosages, with clear and correct explanations about their impact, including the unwanted effects, and with the ultimate decision being made by the individual who will be taking them.

But what we are trying to get across is that it's not so simple as some people would have you think. This is important because, as a manager, it just isn't useful to say, 'Well, if they took their medication, it would all be okay.' The use of medication in an attempt to 'treat' emotions is based upon a belief in the theory of chemical imbalance, which is still contested by many professionals in mental health.

Mental health filters

In our mental health workshops for managers, we educate participants about the concept of 'filters' in mental health. A filter is a specific way that a person makes sense of their world—their life view, if you will. That means that they will come to you with an understanding and an explanation of what life is about, what is happening to them, and what needs to be done, which might be completely opposite to the view you hold. It's all down to your perspective.

It's a natural human trait to want to make sense of the world. As we go through life and experience various things, we build a mental model of cause and effect. It's what we use to figure things out: The reason y happened is x. In this context, it's how we decide: That person is mentally ill because of x, and if we change y and z, they'll get better.

Now, the problem with mental models, especially when they've proved successful for someone, is that they become a *filter* for information and experiences that don't fit their prevailing understanding of the world. Someone else with a very different mental model (or values) can't possibly be right, because experience has shown you that your way works the best. Perhaps their model *could* work, but can you really be bothered thinking about things differently when your way feels so *right?*

Because our life experiences are each so different, these unconscious filters can really get in the way of us understanding and *trusting* each other. So for those of us who don't live alone in a lighthouse, and rely on engaging with others to achieve our goals (i.e. every leader reading this book), being aware of your filter and the filters of others is imperative.

Filters are important because people understand their mental health problem according to the filter they choose. There are probably as many filters as there are people on this earth, but here's how some of the more common variations might describe a mental illness:

Medical

The predominant filter in our Western society is a medical filter. According to this approach, a mental illness is a physical or biological condition.

As we've seen, one theory from the medical filter is that mental illness is a chemical imbalance in the brain. That's the most common explanation that you may have heard of. But, as we've discussed, this is still a theory. If you go to the doctor and describe the symptoms of a mental health problem, they are not able to test for the chemical imbalance—no test exists!

It is likely that there is some kind of chemical imbalance in the brain—after all, every emotion we experience is a chemical imbalance in the brain! We just don't know for sure whether the chemical imbalance causes the emotions of mental ill-health, or if they happen as a result of mental ill-health. Regardless, according to this filter, if you have a chemical imbalance in the brain then it can treated by introducing other chemicals (in the form of medications or drugs) to try to bring you back into balance.

Another medical explanation is that mental illness is genetic. There do appear to be some cases where mental health issues run in families. However, whether this is because of genes or the way someone is raised is sometimes more difficult to identify. It's the nature versus nurture question. And there seems to be evidence for both sides.

Besides medication, another medical treatment for mental health issues is electroconvulsive therapy (ECT), where the person receives an electrical current through the brain. It is usually only used in severe cases of depression, or bipolar and psychotic disorders, where the person has tried all other forms of treatment, which have not been successful. Some people do report improvement after ECT, but many also have problems with memory and thinking after receiving it.

A person with a medical filter may seek treatment for mental health problems through the medical system, by consulting a GP or psychiatrist, taking medication, or even receiving ECT. Recovery in terms of this filter might be viewed as being cured or experiencing a reduction in symptoms.

Spiritual

Now, let's compare that with someone who views the world from a spiritual perspective. Someone with a spiritual filter would say that their mental health problem is not really a medical concern, but is about a loss of connection, meaning or purpose—perhaps a spiritual crisis, loss of faith, or loss of connection to something greater than themselves. In fact, many people who have recovered from mental health problems do describe it this way. They may say that it felt like a breakdown at the time, but, actually, it was a breakthrough. 'I don't want to go back there, but it did help transform me, and make me who I am today.' For many of the hundreds of thousands of people who have recovered from a mental health diagnosis, this filter resonates strongly.

Someone with a spiritual filter would be less likely to describe it as a mental illness, and more likely to talk about emotional distress. They would seek healing, not treatment, through spiritual means. That might mean joining a religion or spiritual group, embracing meditation, prayer or art, or connecting with nature, etc. Recovery in terms of this filter would mean a spiritual breakthrough, finding purpose, connecting with God, etc.

Now, imagine you have someone with a medical filter talking to someone with a spiritual filter about what needs to be done to get them help. They are each going to have very different viewpoints. It's likely that there will be some resistance from both sides.

Psychological

A psychological filter explains mental health problems in terms of thought patterns. Mental disorders might be considered to be distorted or exaggerated thinking patterns that are not useful.

This filter would suggest that if you think negative thoughts all the time, it follows that you are going to feel depressed. Or if you are a perfectionist, with very high standards that you can't always meet, it follows that you will feel anxious about whether you can achieve them or not, and feel disappointed if you don't.

From this perspective, in order to recover from mental health issues, you might seek to change the way you think about things, so that you have more constructive thoughts, which serve you better.

Treatment may be through counselling, psychotherapy, or some kind of talking therapy aimed at assisting the person to change their thought processes. Recovery would mean adopting more useful thinking patterns and coping strategies.

Trauma

This filter is held by the person who would say, 'It's not a chemical imbalance in the brain, and it's not a spiritual crisis, and it's not about my thinking patterns. It's just that I have been through some difficult stuff. Of course, I am having this response. My body, my mind, my psyche—they are just doing what they need to do to cope.'

For a person with a trauma filter, recovery might mean coming to terms with what has happened. They may need to accept that an event has occurred, and focus on how to move forward from here, so their life is no longer impacted in a negative way.

Political

At the extreme, someone who views the world with this filter might say mental disorders don't exist. Instead, what is defined as a mental disorder is subjective, and determined by the norms of any one society at any one point in time. Anyone outside the 'normal' box is considered mentally unwell.

There are actually a lot of eminent psychiatrists who support this view. They call upon the DSM (*The Diagnostic and Statistical Manual*), which we discussed earlier in this chapter, as evidence.

People with a political filter may choose not to participate in the medical, political or social systems. Or they may choose to work within them to advocate for better human rights for people with mental health issues. Recovery might mean gaining more human rights, and being respected as equals, regardless of any individual differences the person has.

Diet and exercise

This is another common filter. Many people say that if we looked after our nutrition and got some exercise, mental health would be much improved. In fact, the research backs this up, showing that exercise is one of the most effective treatments for almost all mental health issues. There is also some more recent research linking mental health problems with certain bacteria in the gut.

Systems

From the systems filter perspective, a mental health problem does not reside in the individual person; it resides in the whole system. For example, it is pretty common to find in child psychology that if a child is having problems, the best approach is to work with the whole family. Interestingly, for adults, an approach that is having very high success rates in Northern Finland, New York and the UK is called 'Open Dialogue'. It is used to help people with psychotic disorders, like schizophrenia, and involves working with the entire family and helping them develop their communication and social networks. This filter also applies to workplaces. Often, it is not just one individual suffering; there may be systems and processes that are not working for many people.

How does all this apply to me as a manager?

The application of the filters for managers is very simple. First, recognise that mental health issues are not 'black and white'. There is a lot of grey and a lot of disagreement. Second, identify what filter (or filters) you may be viewing mental health through. Where did these come from? It is likely a combination of things you have heard throughout your life and experiences you have had with mental health, whether yourself personally or with family members or friends, etc. Notice that they don't necessarily represent the sum total of all human experience! And very rarely is someone's view based on years of study and full-time investigation into the subject matter.

Have your filters changed over time? It is very common for people, including those who have been through a mental health problem, to start with one filter which they hold strongly, but then to swap to another completely, or incorporate another into their perspective as they begin to see the benefits in viewing things a different way.

Think about people around you—the members of your team. Through which filters do you think they view life? And mental health? If you're not sure, a good way to tell is to listen to the type of language they use. Do they use technical, medical language (these people are more likely to adhere to a medical filter) or do they speak about 'life force' and 'healing energy' (these people are more likely to be spiritual)? And so on.

Now, here is the key—once you have a good idea of the filter/s someone else might be using, you can start to communicate with them through that filter, instead of your own. Of course, this doesn't mean that you need to drop your own beliefs about mental health and life, but it does mean that while you are interacting with that person, in order to come together for a positive outcome, you may need to put your filter in the shelf, just for a moment, and see where they are coming from.

After all, imagine if you have a medical filter and you are speaking with someone who holds a spiritual filter. Your suggestion that they see a GP, or take some medication, will be completely out of line with their way of viewing their experience. It would be just the same as if you have a spiritual filter, but are speaking to someone with a medical filter and telling them that what they really need to do is join your religion or undergo a spiritual cleansing ritual. That conversation is just not going to go very far! In the best-case scenario, the person will simply not talk to you about the matter anymore. In the worst-case scenario, it will create increased angst, conflict and distress for both parties.

In fact, we recommend that rather than suggest any particular remedy, which isn't within your role as manager anyway, it is much better to ask the person, 'What do you think is going on?' and 'What do you think might be helpful?" And suspend your judgement of their proposed solution. What really matters to a person in distress is that they feel they have your support, and that they have some next step they can carry out to move forward towards improving their mental and emotional wellbeing. Their next step in recovery will come from whichever filter they are currently in. Trying to force your own filter upon another person simply doesn't help. And if you make a suggestion that doesn't work for them, guess who they're going to blame?

Remember, there is no right or wrong with these filters. They are simply different perspectives, different ways of describing the same thing. There are strengths and weaknesses to each filter, though they may be hard to see when we are too tightly attached to our own.

As a manager, if you can get an understanding of filters, and begin to implement this in your interactions with staff, you are way ahead of the game when it comes to managing the mental health and wellbeing of your team, department or organisation.

2

Identifying Mental Health Issues

A useful tool for thinking about mental health and wellbeing is the mental health continuum.

Imagine a scale, with good, strong, healthy mental health up one end (picture a person who is happy and fulfilled in life, and wakes up every day glad to be alive and excited about the day ahead), and down the other end, the other extreme (someone in severe distress and suffering). You have a range of points along that scale for everyone in between. This is the mental health continuum.

We all fall somewhere on that continuum, and it can change from day to day—sometimes throughout the day. It's not fixed. No one is born at either end. Even someone who is extremely depressed might still find themselves laughing at a funny movie, and for a moment, they have shifted up along the scale. In the middle of the scale is 'normal' (the person who gets up and goes about their day in an 'average' state of mental wellbeing). But have you seen so called 'normal' people on the bus or train on their way to work on a Monday morning? Do they look mentally healthy and happy?

According to the concept of the continuum, somewhere between 'normal' and the 'unwell' end of the scale is a point where people can be diagnosed as suffering from a disorder. As mental health issues cannot be measured, this point of diagnosis—deciding just how bad is bad enough to be classed a mental disorder—comes down largely to the way the person self-reports their experience, and the interpretation made by the 'professional' they are seeing.

Now, consider how this relates to workplaces. When someone is suffering enough to be diagnosed with a mental disorder, they have already reached that point of diagnosis. However, there is a whole group of people, ranging from 'average' and down, who have not actually been diagnosed but who are still experiencing mental distress. There is no name for this group, though people often refer to their experience as 'workplace stress', 'burnout' or just 'stress'.

Interestingly, this terminology seems to be much more acceptable to others than 'mental distress' or 'mental disorder'. But make no mistake, this level of 'stress' is still impacting on the workplace in much the same way as the diagnosable mental health conditions. When someone is moderately anxious, or feeling blue, or suffering from stress, they are not performing their best at work. You, as a manager, are not getting the best out of them. Productivity can suffer, morale can start to drop, and you might see signs of conflict between team members. It's not long before a downward spiral starts.

When we speak with workplaces about mental health, it's not unusual for managers to focus only on the severe end of the scale. If there hasn't been a critical incident, a psychological injury claim, or a suicide, then they often don't think they have a problem—yet. They are banking on there not being an incident. They miss the large number of people experiencing stress and distress who have not yet arrived down the severely unwell end of the scale. And that distress already has a host of negative impacts.

How to spot mental health issues developing

So how can you as a manager spot mental health issues developing? First, let's look at an overview of some of the major categories, so you'll have a basic idea of what people are talking about when they start rolling out the jargon. The medical model does have some utility here, as there do appear to be distinct ways that mental distress can present for people. These can be broken down into broad categories of symptoms, which allow us to communicate about mental health with a bit more insight and understanding. This has value so long as we remember that these are artificial categories. We have never come across a person who fits neatly into just one box when it comes to mental health.

Mental health problems can be divided into two main groups:

- The 'common' mental health issues, like anxiety, depression, psychosis, etc. They are common in the sense that these are more prevalent in society—the types of problems that you are more likely to come across day to day.
- The 'personality disorders', like narcissistic personality disorder or borderline personality disorder. The second group are much more rare, and their definitions even more hotly contested than those of the first group, so we won't spend as much time on them in this book, aside from where it is relevant to a workplace situation.

For the most part, when we are talking about mental health issues, we are referring to the common mental health problems. Within these, you have a couple of broad categories. We'll focus on the following, which are the most prevalent:

- Anxiety
- Depression
- Psychosis
- Substance Use Problems

The descriptions below are not intended to be a comprehensive study of the different disorders—there are plenty of places you can find this information. They are simply intended to give you a bit of an overview of some of the different categories.

Anxiety

Anxiety, like all the emotions of mental distress, is a normal emotion. We all have it, and it is actually a helpful emotion to have. It serves to keep us safe from danger. Anxiety is what makes us look both ways before crossing the street, prepares us to escape dangerous animals, and also helps us to behave in a way that will keep our position within a group of people. I'm sure you've heard of the 'fight or flight response'. Well, anxiety is the emotion that stimulates that response. The underlying emotion is fear.

So when does it become a problem? If you think back to the mental health continuum we discussed, there is a point along that scale at which 'normal' anxiety becomes 'too much' anxiety. That point might be defined differently by different people, but, generally, the experience becomes an anxiety disorder when it is perceived to:

- Be too severe,
- Be too long lasting.

- Interfere with the person's daily activities (particularly work and relationships).
- Occur at an inappropriate time (when there is no obvious danger).

Below is a list of some of the common signs and symptoms of anxiety. We've divided this into physical, psychological and behavioural categories, as well as covering things you might be more likely to see in the workplace context.

Anxiety can be expressed in lots of different ways, so it's unlikely a person is going to experience ALL of these, but the following are some of the common signs and symptoms:

Anxiety

PHYSICAL SIGNS & SYMPTOMS	
Chest pain	Pounding heart
Headaches	Rapid heartbeat
Blushing	Rapid, shallow breathing
Choking, dry mouth	Dizziness
Restlessness	Sweating
Muscle aches and pains	Tingling & numbness
Being unable to settle, physically	Nausea and stomach pains
Sleep problems	Diarrhoea
Tremors & shaking	Vomiting
Changes in appetite	Weight loss or gain
PSYCHOLOGICAL SIGNS & SYMPTOMS	
Unrealistic and excessive worry	High stress
Mind racing or going blank	Nervousness & fear
Decreased concentration	Impatience

Mood swings	Decreased memory
Irritability	Negativity
Confusion	Anger
Feeling on edge, nervous	Sleep disturbance
Extreme sensitivity	Vivid dreams
	Impaired memory

BEHAVIOURAL SIGNS & SYMPTOMS	
Withdrawing socially	Increased drug or alcohol use
Avoiding certain situations	Non suicidal self injury (self harm)
Compulsive behaviour	Constant alertness & watchfulness
Constantly seeking approval	Need to control others, and/or environment
Nervous habits, e.g. pulling hair	Rigidity, Lack of flexibility

Other SIGNS AND SYMPTOMS you may notice in the WORKPLACE:	
Lack of concentration	Absenteeism
Loss of motivation	Presenteeism
Agitation or anger	Over reacting (especially to criticism)
Repeatedly late to work	Conflict with colleagues or clients
Trouble decision making	Late with deadlines
Neglecting responsibilities	Less productive
Micromanagement	Being defensive

Scan the list and you'll start to notice a few things. Firstly, you've probably felt many or all of these at one time or another. Don't worry!

That's normal. Remember, as we said, it is normal and good for you to experience some anxiety. This is not the time to start self-diagnosing!

You may also notice that, generally speaking, when a person is experiencing anxiety, things speed up: their heart rate, breathing, thoughts, perspiration, etc. But you'll also notice areas where the opposite can be the case. For example, when a person is anxious, they may be likely to eat more or less than they usually would, and they may sleep more or less than they usually would. Every individual is different and won't respond to or cope with anxiety in the same way.

There are some different types of anxiety disorder you might have heard of. These distinctions help to further describe different patterns of anxiety that people might have.

Generalised Anxiety Disorder—This is diagnosed when the person is anxious in a wide variety of situations, to the point where it almost seems like it is part of their personality.

Panic Disorder—You've probably heard of panic attacks? A panic attack is when a person goes into a very acute episode of complete panic. The average timespan of a panic attack is about two minutes. They are pretty common and some studies estimate that up to thirty-five per cent of people will have a one-off panic attack at some point in their life. If a person continues to have more panic attacks, and focuses on them so much that they become a central part of their life, then they would likely be diagnosed with panic disorder.

Agoraphobia—When translated literally, this term means 'fear of the marketplace', however, this is deceiving. Agoraphobia is not so much a fear of a place itself, but a fear of having a panic attack there. And so, a person starts avoiding certain places. Common places people avoid are shopping centres, but also public transport, movie cinemas, roads, airports and crowded events. Some people avoid so many places that they may never leave their home.

Specific Phobias—Specific phobias are when a person has a fear of a specific thing. Common phobias include spiders, snakes, chickens, heights, enclosed spaces, blood, needles, clowns, etc. But a person can have a specific phobia of anything.

Social Phobia—This phobia is a bit broader, but generally encompasses a fear of places where people gather. That could be parties, meetings, events with public speaking, etc.

Post Traumatic Stress Disorder (PTSD)—This is the most common of the anxiety disorders, and can be experienced by people who have been through an event which they perceived as being traumatic. Notice we've said 'perceived' as traumatic, rather than 'a traumatic event'. This is a small but crucial distinction. Researchers have long been trying to understand why some people develop PTSD following a challenging event, whereas others don't. For example, following a natural disaster like an earthquake, or similar event where a large number of people are exposed, only a very small proportion will actually go on to develop PTSD. Similarly, despite being in the same war environment, only a relatively small percentage of soldiers develop PTSD.

There are a few factors which are starting to come to light, and one of them is that it depends upon the way the event is perceived. Those who perceived the event as traumatic, and who felt that their lives were in imminent danger, are more likely to develop PTSD. This isn't the only factor, but it is a crucial one. Taking this to the workplace, we need to be careful when we become aware of a colleague who has experienced something that we would normally consider to be traumatic. We need to be careful not impose our own judgement upon the situation. For instance, a colleague arrives at work and explains, 'Look, sorry I was a bit late; I just had a car accident on the way here, and had to stop and get the drivers' details, etc.' It would not be helpful for teammates to overreact, exclaiming, 'Oh my goodness—you must have been terrified!

You could have died! Why don't you take the morning off, so you can recuperate?' The person has not given any indication that they found the event terrifying or that they need special care. By putting these suggestions into the person's head, we can create a problem where there was none. Of course, if the person is saying they feel those things, we can provide support as required. But assuming something is traumatic for someone else is not helpful.

PTSD can be diagnosed when a person shows evidence of three main types of symptom:

1. Being hyper—alert, on edge, jumpy, and reactive. As an example, you may tap them on the shoulder and they jump a mile.
2. Conversely, they often also describe feeling emotionally numb and desensitised to the highs and lows of life. This appears to be a natural coping mechanism.
3. Re-experiencing the event, through flashbacks, nightmares or the like.

Obsessive Compulsive Disorder (OCD)—This is also classed as an anxiety disorder, though it is very rare. Obsessions are the intruding thoughts of distress that a person with OCD has about something. Compulsions are the behaviours or actions that a person performs to cope with the intrusive and distressing thoughts. Common obsessions and compulsions tend to be around:

1. Cleanliness and hygiene, e.g. obsessive thoughts about germs, dirt or getting infected, and compulsive rituals around washing hands a certain number of times, disinfecting everything, or not leaving their house for fear of germs.

2. Safety, e.g. obsessive thoughts about whether they've left the stove on or locked the front door, or about danger on the roads or in public, coupled with compulsive rituals around turning the stove off repeatedly, checking the front door over and over again (perhaps despite being halfway to work each time), or again not leaving the house for fear of danger in public places.

Obviously, OCD can be extremely debilitating for the person experiencing it.

Anxiety is the most common of the mental disorders, affecting around fourteen per cent of the population in any one year. It also tends to be the easiest to overcome, especially if addressed early. However, if not addressed, there is evidence that is can become more severe with time. Often, the person then starts to feel depressed as well. In fact, it is quite common for people to experience both anxiety and depression.

Case Study in Anxiety

Angela is a hard working and dedicated employee. She has a very good work ethic, and takes pride in her accomplishments. Angela always wants to make sure that she is doing everything right, in fact she is a bit of a perfectionist, and that has served her well in the past. The problem is, that lately, Angela has taken on a new project that she is finding quite stressful. Her Manager is very happy with Angela's performance on this project, but Angela is never quite satisfied with her own work. She is staying back late, going over and over the same tasks, and constantly seeking feedback from the Manager to make sure she is doing it right. This is not like her. Angela has noticed that she has trouble going to sleep at night, as her thoughts are racing "what if it isn't good enough?", "what if I forgot to include something?", "what if I got the numbers wrong?", on and on and on. Sometimes she worries so much she gets nauseous, and so she hasn't really felt like eating much lately. She often skips lunch. But, lack of food and sleep also adds to her anxiety and irritability, so when a colleague made a comment on how organised her desk was, she found herself taking it as criticism, and snapped a sharp comment back at him. She felt really bad afterwards, and became quite emotional. She hopes that no one noticed she actually shed a tear or two quietly in her office. Some colleagues have noticed that Angela has been a bit 'on edge' recently, and that she hasn't been joining them for dinner as a team, which she used to love. They are concerned for her because while Angela has always had high standards and been meticulous in her work, she now seems to be going overboard, and is becoming quite distressed.

Depression

Depression, like anxiety, is also a normal emotion. We all feel sad from time to time. That's part of life. But depression can be diagnosed when the sadness is perceived to:

- Be too severe.
- Be too long lasting.
- Interfere with daily activities (especially work and relationships).

Below is a list of some common signs and symptoms of depression:

Depression

PHYSICAL SIGNS & SYMPTOMS	
Fatigue, lack of energy	Sleeping a lot or very little
Headaches	Eating a lot or very little
Muscle aches and pains	Weight loss or gain
Loss of libido	Constipation

Moving Slowly	
PSYCHOLOGICAL SIGNS & SYMPTOMS	
Extreme sadness	Lack or enjoyment in activities previously enjoyed
Feeling worthless	Guilt
Thinking about death, dying, suicide	Anger
Mood swings	Lack of responsiveness
Helplessness	Hopelessness
Self criticism and blame	Negativity
Impaired memory	Lack of concentration
Trouble decision making	Confusion
BEHAVIOURAL SIGNS & SYMPTOMS	
Withdrawing socially	Increased drug or alcohol use
Neglecting Responsibilities	Non suicidal self injury (self harm)
Loss of interest in personal appearance	Loss of motivation
Other SIGNS AND SYMPTOMS you may notice in the WORKPLACE:	
Repeatedly late to work	Absenteeism
Late with deadlines	Presenteeism
Agitation or anger	Over reacting (especially to criticism)
Being defensive	Conflict with colleagues or clients
Less productive	

In the list, you'll notice a couple of things again. Firstly, in comparison to anxiety, depression is characterised by slowing down—fatigue, lack of energy, moving slowly, speaking slowly, slowed thinking and decision-making, etc. But, again, everyone will experience it differently so even if you've had your own bout of depression, it doesn't mean it is the same for anyone else.

Major Depressive Disorder—This is the main type of depression, and it is described as a pervasive and persistent low mood that is accompanied by low self-esteem and by a loss of interest or pleasure in normally enjoyable activities. A person may be diagnosed with major depressive disorder if the symptoms persist for more than two weeks, and if they impact on the person's functioning in work or relationships.

Bipolar Disorder—Bipolar is sometimes categorised under the 'depression' umbrella. Previously called 'manic depressive disorder', a person diagnosed with bipolar disorder experiences periods of time when they feel depressed, and also periods of time with a very elevated mood. The elevated mood is significant and is known as mania. During mania, an individual feels or acts abnormally happy, energetic or irritable. They often make poorly-thought-out decisions with little regard to the consequences. The need for sleep is usually reduced. In some cases, the person can become so manic that they can experience an episode of psychosis. The period of 'mania' can last anywhere from a few hours to a few days or a week, and is followed by a sharp decline into depression.

Self-harm—Self-harm isn't a diagnosis as such, but it is a coping mechanism people sometimes use when experiencing depression (or even anxiety). Self-harm means any behaviour which involves the deliberate causing of pain or injury to oneself. It can include cutting, burning or hitting oneself, pulling skin or hair, interfering with wounds healing, putting objects under the skin, ingesting poisonous substances, binge-eating or starvation, or repeatedly putting oneself in dangerous situations. It can also involve abuse of drugs or alcohol, including overdosing on prescription medications. People harm themselves for a number of reasons, including to cope with painful feelings, to feel 'alive' or end feelings of numbness and dissociation, to seek help, to punish themselves, and to avoid suicidal feelings. When someone self-harms, they do not intend to commit suicide (though sometimes they might die by accident).

Suicide—Suicide is also not a diagnosis, but it is most commonly related to depression. Suicide is when a person intentionally takes their own life. It is important to distinguish this from an accidental death (e.g. in the case of a drug overdose or car accident) and from euthanasia (where a person assists in ending the life of another). People who have attempted suicide often explain that while they didn't necessarily want to die, they wanted to end their suffering, and, therefore, they took action to end their life.

Case Study in Depression

Tom is a friendly, intelligent and sociable guy. He split up with his long term partner a few months ago, and since then his manager Julie, has noticed that he hasn't really gotten over it yet. Break ups can be difficult, so she expected Tim to be a bit down for a while, but it doesn't seem to be getting any better. In fact, it seems to be getting worse. Tim is not participating and avoiding group activities, projects and meetings. Slowly but surely he has stopped taking care of his appearance, and he is actually starting to look a bit shabby. He is turning up to work later and later, and has started calling in sick more often than the usual. He seems to have lost all enthusiasm for his work, and tends to forget things that she told him just yesterday. He looks like he is just going through the motions, and team mates are starting to get annoyed at his negativity and his moping around. Julie is worried about Tim, but doesn't want to say anything in case she makes it worse.

Psychosis

Psychosis is often described as a state where someone 'loses contact with reality'. It is important to note, however, that the experience is very real for that person. In fact, the language 'losing touch with reality' is not considered best practice at present, because it displays a lack of sensitivity and respect for the person's experience. Instead, we tend to think of psychosis as 'altered perceptions'.

Using this definition, we can observe that, just like with anxiety and depression, we all at times experience some altered perceptions. For example, have you ever been walking down the street and thought you heard someone call your name? Perhaps you even turned around to find them. Don't worry. That's not psychosis; it's normal. But it is an experience of altered perception. Or maybe you were searching through the cupboard for the salt—you knew it was there, but you just couldn't see it. Someone else showed you where it was—right in front of you the whole time. And what about *de ja vu*—that strange feeling of having already experienced something? There are all mini-examples of when our perception is altered. The mind is an amazing and mysterious piece of equipment!

Altered perception can be diagnosed as psychosis when it is perceived to:

- Be too severe.
- Be too long lasting.
- Interfere with daily activities (especially work and relationships).

We saw previously that when someone experiences anxiety for a period of time, it can become more severe and in some cases lead to depression. The same is true for psychosis. It is rare, but sometimes when depression becomes very severe, people can start to experience altered perceptions which could be diagnosed as psychosis. It is thought that this is a protective mechanism.

Two common symptoms of psychosis are:

1. Unusual Perceptual Experiences (Hallucinations)—The person may see things that others around them do not see, hear things that others don't hear, or feel things that they cannot see.
2. Unusual Beliefs (Delusions)—The person may hold very unusual beliefs, which others around them do not have evidence for. Common beliefs which may be considered unusual are:
   a. Beliefs of grandeur—The person may believe they are a religious figure, a celebrity, or that they are destined to become a person of note.
   b. Beliefs of persecution—The person may believe they are being chased or attacked, for example, by neighbours, the mafia, police, aliens or spies.

Other signs and symptoms are listed in the table below:

Psychosis

PHYSICAL SIGNS & SYMPTOMS	
Unusual perceptual experiences	Change in appetite
Change in energy	Sleep disturbance
PSYCHOLOGICAL SIGNS & SYMPTOMS	
Depression	Anxiety
Irritability	Suspiciousness and paranoia
Flat or inappropriate emotion	Difficulty concentrating or paying attention
Feeling different to others	Odd or unusual ideas
BEHAVIOURAL SIGNS & SYMPTOMS	
Social withdrawal and isolation	Increased drug or alcohol use
Neglecting responsibilities	Loss of motivation
Other SIGNS AND SYMPTOMS you may notice in the WORKPLACE:	

Repeatedly late to work	Absenteeism
Late with deadlines	Presenteeism
Agitation or anger	Over reacting (especially to criticism)
Being defensive	Conflict with colleagues or clients
Less productive	

There are many different categories and subcategories of psychosis, but the following are some of the main diagnoses you might have heard of:

Schizophrenia—The term comes from the Greek for 'fractured mind', which refers to the changes and distortions in thinking and perception that people with schizophrenia commonly experience. It is not a case of 'split personality'. A person diagnosed with schizophrenia may experience unusual perceptual experiences, unusual beliefs, unclear or confused thinking and language, reduced social engagement, or unusual emotional expression. There is usually significant disruption to all areas of the person's life.

Schizoaffective disorder—The easiest way to describe this diagnosis is as a combination of schizophrenia and a mood disorder, either depression or bipolar disorder.

Drug Induced Psychosis—This occurs where psychosis can be clearly attributed to substance use. It is a psychosis that results from the poisonous effects of chemicals or drugs, including those produced by the body itself and medications.

Case Study in Psychosis

Eric is a new employee who joined the team about 6 months ago. Eric has always been pretty quiet and kept to himself, but he does a good enough job, and his Manager Joe is happy with his work. Over the past two months, Joe and Eric have been able to spend more time together in the field, and have gotten to know each other a bit more. During these conversations, Joe has sometimes noticed that Eric has some pretty unusual ideas about things. He would say he is a bit of a conspiracy theorist. That's fine, but lately Eric has started to tell Joe about his concerns that his neighbours are spying on him. Joe laughed it off at first, but Eric is becoming more and more distressed, and telling him complicated stories about interactions he has had with his neighbours and other people in the community. Joe has tried to offer some suggestions but it doesn't seem to have helped Eric much. And Joe notices that often these stories are getting more and more incredible (and unlikely) and just don't seem to add up. He even contradicts himself at times. At the same time, Joe has noticed some discrepancies in the reports he has been getting from Eric and from other team members about their progress on certain projects. When he asked Eric about this, Eric accused the other team members of wanting to sabotage him, and said they are all out to get him. When Joe's asked for evidence, there's always a reason as to why the evidence can't be collected. Joe wants to give Eric the benefit of the doubt, but there are more and more things that just don't seem right. Yesterday Joe noticed Eric seemed very agitated, and was muttering to himself while working on a project. When Joe approached him, he didn't even seem to recognise Joe at first and even looked to be a bit scared of him for a few moments. Joe feels like he's out of his depth.

Substance Use Disorder

Like the other disorders described above, substance use disorder is not just the use of substances. We all use some kinds of substances sometimes, whether it's alcohol, medications, or even caffeine or sugar!

Substance use disorder is diagnosed when the use of one or more substances leads to significant impairment or distress, or the use of the drug has detrimental effects on the individual's physical and mental health, or the welfare of others.

Substances which can have this effect include psychoactive drugs, which are available both illegally, such as cocaine, heroin, marijuana and amphetamines, and legally, such as medications, alcohol or tobacco.

It is common for people with substance use disorder to use drugs in an attempt to cope with underlying mental health problems. For that reason, there is much debate as to whether Substance Use Disorder should exist as a mental disorder in and of itself, or whether it is a coping mechanism similar to self-harm.

Case Study in Substance Use

Paul is a very caring and supportive workmate. He is very dependable and always has time to help out his colleagues, or listen to them when they need to debrief. His manager Amy has noticed though that lately he has seemed very tired, and a bit distracted at work. Paul actually called in sick last Monday as he said he was still recovering from a nasty cold. She figured he must be a bit run down—it is the season for it after all. He was sick again on Friday too. The next time Amy met with Paul, they were going through some notes together, and she thought she noticed a very faint smell of alcohol, but she didn't say anything. Over the next few weeks Amy started to notice Paul was making some mistakes in his work—nothing major, but he just didn't seem to be paying attention to the details. He has also started to complain a lot about Mondays, which he never used to do before. The reason why Amy liked Paul so much as an employee is because he always had a great attitude. But, he has been coming into work late a few times, and it looks like he is starting to grow a beard and his shirts don't look well pressed either. Amy is starting to think something is going on, but she isn't sure what, as Paul is pretty private about his personal life.

Personality Disorders

Personality disorders are considered as being a different category to the 'common' mental disorders. The following are some of the more well known personality disorders:

Antisocial Personality Disorder—People diagnosed with antisocial personality disorder are usually referred to as 'sociopaths'. To be diagnosed, they must, before the age of fifteen, have displayed repeated violations of the law, pervasive lying and deception, physical aggressiveness, reckless disregard for the safety of themselves or others, consistent lack of responsibility in work and family, and lack of remorse.

Psychopathy—Psychopathy can be considered a more severe version of antisocial personality disorder, but it does have some differences. A psychopath also displays a lack of empathy and is unable to form emotional bonds. They will use manipulation and charm to achieve their outcome, with no regard for the consequences. They are capable of controlling their emotions and mimicking feelings to fit in with society, whereas a sociopath is less organised and more likely to act inappropriately spontaneously. A psychopath will have complete lack of guilt or remorse, whereas a sociopath may have remorse if they have hurt someone close to them. The word 'psychopath' is thrown round a lot but the disorder is, in fact, very rare.

Borderline Personality Disorder—This is diagnosed when a person shows a long-term and consistent pattern of unstable moods and emotions. The person also has a poor sense of self, difficulty forming long-lasting relationships, and can be reckless.

Narcissistic Personality Disorder—People with this disorder show a long-term pattern of preoccupation with themselves, excessive self-importance, and a total lack of empathy for others. They have an extreme sense of superiority.

Other personality disorders include: Dependent Personality Disorder, Avoidant Personality Disorder, Histrionic Personality Disorder, Paranoid Personality Disorder, Schizoid Personality Disorder, Schizotypal Personality Disorder, and Obsessive Compulsive Personality Disorder (different to OCD).

As you read these descriptions, you may start to think of people you know who display one or more of the signs. A word of caution—just as we saw with the 'common' mental disorders, we could all experience some of these symptoms from time to time to a lesser degree. Despite the language of personality disorders being used more and more readily these days, and there being much in the popular media about personality disorders, they are extremely rare. It is not generally helpful to think of your staff (or your boss!) as having these personality disorders. And remember, even the professionals still debate whether there is any validity in personality disorders anyway.

But what if they're hiding it?

You'll notice as you look at these lists that a lot of the things listed are 'internal'—things that the person may be thinking or feeling, but wouldn't necessarily show on the outside. These are the 'symptoms'. Then there are the 'signs'; the things that you as an observer may be able to see, like if the person is trembling physically, or is slumped over in their posture.

It is true that a lot of people will go to a lot of effort not to show any outward signs of what is going on for them on the inside. This can be for a whole range of reasons, but usually it comes down to the person being afraid—of being judged negatively, of what others might think, of the impact it would have on their career, family, etc.

In these cases, it can be very hard for observers to identify that a person might be struggling with their mental health. There is no fool-proof way around this, but here are our recommendations:

1. Pay attention. When you are visiting friends or seeing colleagues, take the time to be present with them, notice their appearance and listen to how they speak. Too often, we are so caught up in our own busy lives and To Do lists that we don't see the signs that are actually right in front of us.

2. Don't judge others. If people see you judging others, they will, of course, expect that you are likely to judge them too. And to avoid that, they will go to extra lengths to put on a mask and pretend everything is okay. This is especially the case in the workplace, where your judgements as a manager carry more weight, and can mean the difference between getting the promotion or not.

3. Show you care. Build meaningful relationships with people, so you come to know what is 'normal' for them. This builds your 'sensory acuity', so you are more tuned in to slight changes in their demeanour. Change is one of the key warning signs that all may not be well.

4. Be real. If you're not having a great day, it's okay to say, 'Well, actually, I'm not having a great day'. This lets people know they don't have to be perfect all the time. We seem to have an expectation that everyone is 120 per cent happy and successful all the time. We assume this because we see their lives everyday on social media! Of course, those are just the selected highlights, but we sometimes forget that. Being a manager, our staff can often feel that we have it all together (little do they know!), and that they have to perform to exceptionally high standards, and be happy about it all the time. When you think about it—that's ludicrous! We all have our down days.

How do you know if they're faking it?

This is the question that most managers who attend our courses want to know the answer to, but don't know how to ask. 'How do I know if it's truly a mental health problem, or if they're just manipulating me to get something out of this situation?'

It's an impossible question. And not a very helpful one. Here's why:

As we've seen, diagnosis is symptom based. If someone goes to see a doctor or a psychologist, that professional will make a determination based, ultimately, on their personal judgement about what the person tells them. Even when the clinician has doubts about what the person is saying, who's to say they're not telling the truth? Clearly, if they have ended up in a consulting room, then there must be something going on. And so a diagnosis will be made.

If the person has done a little bit of homework, and describes a couple of symptoms of mental distress, then they are extremely likely to walk away with a certificate and an official diagnosis. Then, for all intents and purposes, they 'have' a mental health condition and need to be treated accordingly at work. However, even if the person is manipulating the situation, it suggests that there is something really not working between them and the workplace environment (or manager) for them to feel the need to do such a thing.

In reality, this isn't a useful question for managers to keep thinking about because there are many, many more people who are suffering but pretending to be okay than there are people who abuse the system. Changing our whole system for the rare one per cent of people who might take advantage of it is not helping anybody. It is much better to create a supportive and positive working environment which fosters good mental health.

For all these reasons, it's better not to ask the question. It doesn't change the best way in which to respond to issues of mental health, which we'll turn to in part two.

Can people recover?

The concept of 'recovery' from mental health problems has been around for a long time now. In fact, it can be found in psychiatric texts from over a century ago. However, this is still a question that pops up from time to time in our work with organisations.

We believe that people have been conditioned to think that a mental health problem is a permanent condition, largely because of the medical filter which has been and still is predominant in our society. You see, if a person's mental health condition is thought of as a physical illness, it stands to reason that short of some kind of physical intervention, it won't get any better. Couple that with our experiences (either personal or through movies, TV and the media) of people who have severe mental health conditions, who are portrayed as 'the mad man', 'the lunatic' or the 'village nutter'. Apart from a few scattered text books kept hidden in some dusty libraries, the majority of medical professionals for most of the 20th century did believe that: 'once crazy, always crazy'. As you read earlier, they did take people in mental distress off the streets into big institutions, but the idea was to medicate (usually for the main purpose of sedation) and wait, with the expectation that the person would live out the rest of their life in the psychiatric hospital. A lot of the medications used in that time period were very toxic, and for those people who are still alive now, often what appear to be the signs of mental illness are, in fact, the effects of brain damage and trauma.

This was the status quo up until about the 1960s and 1970s, when things started to change. There was a global movement of deinstitutionalisation, where it was thought people might have a better quality of life if they were integrated into and cared for within the community, rather than in hospital settings. The initial plan was for the money invested in public hospitals to be redirected to community care facilities. People were moved out and hospitals shut down, but, unfortunately, the money and support didn't follow, which led to homelessness and a host of other social problems.

At the same time, people who had recovered from mental health issues started to come forward and tell their stories of recovery. Since then, a huge body of anecdotal evidence has amassed globally from people sharing what it took for them to recover their mental health. When people say, 'It's not possible to recover—where's the proof?' they say 'I'm the proof!'

We also have quantitative data. Numerous research studies and meta-analyses have demonstrated that even in the most severe of cases and conditions, a large proportion of people do recover from mental health problems. These studies have been conducted around the world, with thousands of people, over the last fifty years. They basically involve recording the details of people with severe mental health issues like schizophrenia and other psychotic disorders, and then following them up ten, fifteen or twenty years later to see how many have recovered. What is found again and again is that around fifty-five to sixty per cent of people completely recover—even from those very severe mental health conditions. And the numbers are even better for depression and anxiety, especially in the mild to moderate categories, and especially when people get help early.

Note that, so far, we've been speaking with the assumption that 'recovery' means a complete cure. And for many people, it does, but there is also another type of recovery called 'personal recovery'. This refers to the person who might still experience symptoms of mental distress from time to time, or perhaps they may still be taking some medication, but they are no longer in the deep hole they were in before. They have recovered their sense of meaning and fulfilment in life. They might not describe themselves as 'all better' or 'cured', but they go about their daily life and have a sense of purpose.

Whichever way you look at it, the answer to the question 'can people recover?' is a resounding yes! Absolutely. And now that we have that established, mental health professionals around the world are being trained in 'what works' for helping people to recover. Unfortunately, some countries and pockets are clinging on to old ways of treating people, and taking a little longer to change their ways, but those adopting a 'recovery-oriented' approach are getting very good results.

This recovery-orientated approach entails emphasising and supporting a person's potential for recovery. This is a key focus at the Workplace Mental Health Institute, where we believe recovery is not only possible, but probable. Our approach also recognises that a person experiencing mental distress has strengths, skills and personal characteristics despite their current emotional state, and keeps the focus on ability rather than disability.

The authors are considered experts in this recovery-oriented approach and have spent years training clinicians in the established principles and techniques. These are the same principles and techniques which we are now applying to workplace settings. Of course, in the workplace, it is not the manager's role to be a counsellor or therapist (more on that later), but the principles such as 'respect', 'dignity' and 'choice' are most certainly applicable.

This is particularly important right now because mental health issues in the workplace appear to be getting worse. Not only that, but they come with a great cost—for the organisations that people work for as well as the people experiencing mental distress themselves. This is what we'll look at next.

3

The Costs and Causes of Worsening Mental Health in the Workplace

I s our mental health getting worse? Or are we just hearing a lot more about it these days?

Let's have a look at the numbers.

We know that mental health issues are highly prevalent around the world. The statistics tell us that one in four adults will experience a mental disorder each year. Across a lifetime, around fifty per cent of people will experience a mental disorder at some point in their life. That's half of us! And that's not just your regular garden-variety 'stress'. Everyone experiences stress sometimes, and that's normal. These are the statistics for *mental disorder*, when stress isn't experienced and overcome, but gets so bad that it impacts negatively on the person's life in a long-lasting way. Not necessarily all of these people go and get a diagnosis, or seek help, and that's something else to take into consideration. There is a lot of suffering out there, and a lot of people going it alone.

Meanwhile, rates of prescriptions for mental disorders are increasing exponentially. The United States is possibly the worst offender: More than one in five adults (twenty-six per cent of women and fifteen per cent of men) were on at least one mental health medication in 2010, up twenty-two per cent from ten years earlier. An OECD report put Canada at number three in the world and Australia at number two in their use of antidepressants. And the UK has seen a 7.5 per cent increase in the prescription of psychiatric medications between 2013 to 2015, up 500 per cent since 1992.

Then there's suicide. Globally, over 800,000 people take their life each year. That is one person every forty seconds, many of whom are full-time workers. It is not unusual for our team to go to a workplace and have the manager tell us that, in the last few weeks, they have had a colleague who has taken their life. It's fairly common. When we ask groups we work with how many people know someone who has suicided, about seventy-five per cent of the room will raise their hand. This doesn't even take into account the number of people who have attempted suicide, which is about thirty times the suicide rate, and those who have seriously contemplated it, but not taken action. This is serious stuff. Suicide is far too common and, yet, we don't really talk about it much.

In many Western countries, despite the increasing awareness of suicide, mental health and wellbeing, we are seeing these numbers getting worse. I can't help thinking that if this were the flu or some physical ailment, then we would be paying more attention. The only credible way to describe this situation is epidemic.

How are workplace issues contributing?

While the reasons for declining mental health are varied and complex, we have found time and time again that the following concerns underlie a lot of the workplace-induced mental health issues:

Intensification of work

It's no secret that we're working longer hours and being expected to take on more responsibility. The volume of work is enormous and relentless. On top of this, the level of knowledge required to stay current in a role or profession is increasing exponentially. Many people have chronic mental fatigue and adrenal burnout caused by prolonged stress, poor diet and exercise habits, and too much alcohol and caffeine. Untreated, chronic stress is a precursor to mental disorder, and an aggravating factor for an existing condition.

Pace of organisational change

Organisational change is a fact of life in today's organisations. Our desire for better products cheaper and faster means that organisations have to move quickly to capture or maintain market share. Silicon Valley continues to show us that two guys in a garage can disrupt entire established industries almost overnight. Growing organisations have fast paced cultures with a high level of intensity; declining companies experience job insecurity and anxiety; acquiring and merging companies experience clashes of culture as established cultural patterns and power structures are thrown into chaos. This all results in a constantly unstable and unfamiliar environment for employees.

Environmental uncertainty

As if there wasn't enough change in organisations, we currently have an economy and environment in flux. Recent high profile closures in the manufacturing industry not only cause anxiety and uncertainty in those industries, but in the supply chains and adjacent industries that rely on them. Climate change continues to make its presence felt in the form of natural disasters, which have a significant economic and social impact. The economics force many organisations into downsizing and restructuring, causing employment uncertainty for many individuals, and increased workloads for no extra pay for those who do keep their jobs.

What is this costing the workplace?

How are the ensuing mental health issues affecting workplaces? One of the most obvious areas is psychological injury claims, which are rising.

Did you know that the average cost to an organisation for a successful psychological injury claim is now over $250,000? For employees successfully demonstrating that their employer is the cause of or main contributor to their mental disorder, this is the average payout they can expect. The amount is calculated on the basis of direct payments and increased premiums, so you can add to that any legal fees and the cost of replacing the employee. In Australia, there was a recent landmark case that resulted in a payout of $1 million dollars to a lady who had developed a mental disorder as a result of bullying in the workplace. This tells you just how seriously mental health matters are being taken by the courts.

We are also seeing incredibly high rates of mental health related absenteeism, with the average worker taking 3.2 days of 'stress leave' each year. When an employee feels so stressed or burned out or disengaged that they take a sick day, even though they're not 'physically sick', the organisation is hit with a double whammy—not only do they pay the employee's normal wage as a sick leave entitlement, but they incur the opportunity cost of the work the employee would have contributed that day. How much money might the employee have saved the business or made the business that day, had they felt motivated and capable of coming to work? We hear the term 'mental health day' used in a tongue-in-cheek way, but this masks a very real phenomenon when otherwise motivated and engaged employees need to 'pull a sickie' to regroup and recharge so they can make it to work the next day.

It's worse for employees with depression, who will, it's estimated, take three to four days off each month. That's one day a week! Twenty per cent of their productivity is gone, just like that. This results in an average cost of $9,660 per year per worker in absenteeism alone.

That's not all. The losses from presenteeism are found to be even higher, up to six times the cost of absenteeism. Presenteeism is like absenteeism, except the person turns up for work. While they're there, their mind isn't in the game. They might stare at their screen in a trance; read the same report over and over again because it's not sinking in; make mistakes that result in rework and wasted time; or procrastinate because they don't have the mental energy to work on anything high-priority. In some cases we've heard of, they're literally sleeping on the job! Studies by Medibank Private (The Cost of Workplace Stress, 2007) estimate that whatever a company is losing in absenteeism, they can multiply it by six times to account for the hidden cost of presenteeism.

When an employee goes over the brink and decides the only option available to them is to resign, there is a hidden cost equivalent to their full annual salary to replace them. That amount consists of the cost of rehiring, the cost of training the new hire, and the opportunity cost while the new person is coming up to speed. That is if the organisation does replace them. Some organisations make the situation worse for themselves by distributing the extra work to other team members, which leads to more of the same—stress-related burnout and attrition.

Mental health issues cause an increase in workplace conflict and claims of bullying and harassment, not to mention performance management and human resource issues. It has been estimated that over seventy per cent of all human resources problems in the workplace are actually the result of underlying mental health issues. Many HR managers we talk to say that's an understatement!

Finally, there's morale. On the whole, workers are disengaged, dissatisfied and disempowered. Many feel they are dependent on their job, and they feel like there is no way out. Of course, some workplaces are wonderful. In fact, they are known around the world for being unique. But that's just the problem—they are few and far between. Most workplaces are in trouble, real trouble.

We've seen that things are getting worse. But we've also seen that awareness has increased. This begs the question: Why is workplace mental health getting worse, despite our efforts in this area?

We've seen that mental health is getting worse generally, but there are some specific factors at play when it comes to the workplace...

How are organisations and educators making things worse?

The problem of mental health is compounded by many of the mental health education programs that organisations put in place to try and address the issue. The trouble is not that workplaces are introducing education—that's great! The trouble is that they are implementing the wrong type of education.

Again, it's not deliberate. Most people who don't work in the mental health industry wouldn't even realise that there are different types of education or approaches to mental health. They would see all education as equal. But we know better. There are a variety of issues with the approaches taken by organisations and their educators in this area. Here are the main five:

#1 Teaching sickness opposed to wellness

We believe one of the reasons we are seeing workplace mental health issues getting worse, despite increasing attention being paid to them, is that employees are being taught how to do 'sickness' instead of how to do 'wellness'. Typically, an organisation will decide to run some 'awareness' sessions, the aim being to make everyone aware that mental health issues exist, and that it is okay to talk about it at work. Sounds good in theory, but, too often, they bring in a so-called mental health professional who describes the various types of mental disorders and provides a checklist of signs and symptoms. Pretty soon, everyone leaves the session having ticked off most of the list, diagnosing themselves with anxiety or depression. The next thing is that they start to behave as if they have these disorders—calling in sick, claiming they are stressed, and complaining about their workload.

One might say that the 'awareness session' had the intended result—now, people are talking about mental disorder. But I doubt this is the outcome the organisation really wanted for the business. Now, we're not suggesting that organisations should continue to do nothing. That's not the solution either. But they need to become more discerning when it comes to whom they choose to deliver the messages about mental health and wellbeing, and how the messages are communicated.

This is the difference between delivering mental health education using a purely 'medical' approach versus the recovery-oriented approach I mentioned in the last chapter.

It comes down to a difference in the language used in the delivery of these sessions, but it makes ALL the difference in the outcome achieved. You want your staff to leave an awareness session feeling informed about what it looks like when things go wrong, but also feeling empowered with the belief that they can prevent, minimise and handle any mental health challenges that may come their way.

It's the difference between hearing your air host/ess saying, 'In the unlikely event of an emergency, here's what we do…' versus: 'We could fall out of the sky with no warning…" Which do you think sends the better message?

#2 'Anyone any time' messages

Along the same vein, unfortunately, in an attempt to de-stigmatize mental health, many educators go so far as to tell people that 'it can happen to anyone at any time'. While we agree that no one is immune, this is an exaggeration of the point. We agree that mental ill-health does not discriminate according to IQ or economic status or any other such variable, but there are conditions, both environmental and psychological, which are known to create an environment ripe for mental health issues to develop. Equally, there are conditions which can prevent and protect against the development of mental health issues. So it doesn't strike just anyone unawares, as the case is sometimes presented.

The problem with the 'anyone any time' message is that it can create a sense of fear and uncertainty in people, to the point where not all but many employees may start to doubt themselves and their emotions, and become hyper vigilant for anything that just might indicate a mental health problem. This is incredibly disempowering.

Not only that, but the message is that once you 'get it' (as if it were a virus), there is not much you can do about it. This is also a very disempowering message to receive.

#3 Poorly executed activities

Another thing that can make workplace mental health programs fail, or even worsen the mental health of the employees, are well meaning but poorly executed workplace mental health activities. One common example we've seen is kind-hearted managers and HR directors deciding to promote mental health with an annual event, usually round October, which is Mental Health Month in most parts of the globe. The typical activity is to put on a morning tea (if we feed them, they will come). They scatter a few brochures around the place about counselling services, and perhaps someone even says a few words about mental health. Everyone stands around, talks with each other about how important the topic is, and perhaps mentions a cousin of theirs who was depressed, or worse—has schizophrenia. Management then pats themselves on the back and no one mention mental health again for another year.

Now, in some organisational cultures, that works out just fine. But in many workplaces, particularly those with a stigmatised view of mental health, or where employees are already disgruntled with management for some other reason, that kind of thing can be seen as very tokenistic, and that works against the ultimate aim of the activity. We've heard employees say, 'Management don't care about our wellbeing. Sure, they put on a morning tea, but if they really cared, they'd do something about our sixty-hour work-week' (or our pay rate, or KPIS, or whatever else their grudge may be). And they're right.

Similarly, running a short education program as a one-off to 'tick the box', rarely provides the type of change an organisation would benefit from. To get real results, you need to give it some time, attention and resources on a consistent basis. Not necessarily huge amounts, but enough, and at the right times. As you'll see in part two, integrating our workplace mental health activities within the organisational systems is vital.

#4 Fear and risk aversion

One of the main reasons why workplace mental health is getting worse is that it is often approached in a purely risk-averse way. Mental health issues are seen as a problem to be avoided. In fact, many organisations put the 'mental health' topic down as the responsibility of their 'Risk Management' or 'Health & Safety' department, as opposed to their 'People and Culture' or 'Human Resources' department. In our view, there are a myriad of different elements to take into consideration. It is important in mental health that we are not just focused on avoiding the worst-case scenarios, but that we also look at how we can develop the mental strength and resilience of the workforce. When organisations approach mental health from a space of fear, the activities they choose to do position mental *disorder* as a problem to be addressed, and minimised, as opposed to positioning mental *health* as a positive thing to be celebrated and strengthened.

#5 Providing 'awareness' but not real skills

Awareness is a good start, and sometimes it is what is needed to start to shift a culture which traditionally hasn't spoken about mental health or wellbeing. But it's not enough. A brief session which makes everyone aware of the issue does nothing to improve the way it is handled within an organisation. It does nothing to build the personal resilience of the participants. Even if the awareness session includes some direction for where to get help, the underlying message often conveyed to staff is: 'If you have a problem, it's your responsibility (fault), and you should go and get it fixed here.' Of course, that's not the intention, but that is the message that can be received. It stops short of teaching staff how to actually approach a colleague if they are concerned for their wellbeing, or teaching managers how to handle the tricky issues which can arise when it comes to mental health and, furthermore, how to create a mentally healthy workplace in the first place. That cannot be taught in a brief 'information' or 'awareness' session.

#6 Treating mental disorder like physical illness

This just doesn't work. When a mental health concern does become apparent, organisations are hamstrung by a physical injury model that recommends the employee be sent home until they're feeling better. Provided the workplace itself is not the problem, many people with mental distress express a desire to keep working while they work through their mental health issue, and from a clinical perspective, work provides many benefits conducive to recovery (like daily structure and something to focus on other than the distress). But, instead, we are sending people home to an environment where the person is likely to ruminate on the matter, and start thinking all sorts of unhelpful things: 'I couldn't hack it at work,' 'I bet they think I'm completely crazy,' 'I can never face them again,' 'I'm useless,' and so on. The mental health problem is bound to be exacerbated. Of course, for some people, a break from work is exactly what is needed, but on the whole, the research indicates that outcomes are better for people when they can stay in work in some capacity.

When we treat mental health issues like we would a physical illness, we are likely to send the person to the doctor, and request a medical certificate to prove their illness. As discussed, when it comes to mental health conditions, the very nature of the issue is mental, not physical, so there is no conclusive blood test or brain scan or any other diagnostic tool that can be put into play. Diagnosis is instead made on the basis of the person's self-reported symptoms—their feelings and thoughts—and the clinician's judgement.

Not only does a diagnosis tend to delay recovery (receiving a diagnosis of a mental disorder delays recovery by up to five years, on average), it also places the person in the position of having to prove they are unwell. That kind of thinking can *make* a person unwell. Just like the medical student who starts reading about all sorts of rare illnesses can start to think maybe they have them, we can make ourselves mentally unwell by concentrating on our distress and focusing on the feelings so we can prove them to our GP or to our workplace. We don't like to be thought of as dishonest, so our mind creates or worsens the symptoms in order to prove our veracity.

Treating mental health issues at work in the same way you would physical illnesses does not help the individual and usually leads to a drain on the team and the organisation.

The overriding problem is that, when it comes to workplace mental health, organisations are new at this. We don't yet have another model to rely upon. That is what needs to be developed.

How are managers making things worse?
The above approaches at an organisation level can't help but filter down to management, so the answer to this question in many ways echoes the answer to the last. There's more, however. Over the years working with organisations, we've seen a number of strategies employed by managers to address employee mental health concerns. As you can imagine, these strategies sit on a continuum from effective to frankly counterproductive. Of the latter, we've compiled the top seven fatal mistakes managers make when it comes to employee mental health:

#1 Assuming mental health problems are isolated
Many workplaces adopt a reactive posture to mental health problems. They may be aware of a few problems—some individuals—who are struggling or who are 'a bit high maintenance' or who even have gone so far as to lodge psychological injury claims. The organisation deals with these 'isolated' cases by sending the person on stress leave, and perhaps for good measure, decides to run some 'awareness' sessions for employees.

Mental health problems in the workplace resemble the well worn iceberg analogy: the problems you know about are only the tip of a much larger iceberg that is a drain on your organisation's morale and productivity, and a ready supply of future workplace mental health challenges.

The statistics tell us that one in five adult Australians each year experience a mental disorder. The ones you know about are the proverbial 'canaries in the coal mine'. The silent majority is just that: silent.

When preparing an organisational response to employee mental health problems, consider deeper and more integrated strategies than the easy but ineffective in the long term 'stress leave and awareness sessions' approach.

#2 Further isolating the person

It's all too common that when a staff member starts showing signs that they are not mentally well, their manager will decide they have to tread carefully, and so they'll seek advice on what to do next. They'll speak with their own manager, and also HR, who may then discuss things among themselves and perhaps involve Legal... By the time the staff member with the (potential) problem is approached, decisions have been made by multiple parties, none of whom are in possession of the facts—because no one has spoken to the staff member in question.

If you were that staff member, learning that several people had discussed your mental state behind your back and come to some decisions without involving you, how likely would you be to trust your manager or any of those people again?

One of the first things, if not the very first thing, that suffers when people become distressed and mentally unwell is real trust in the relationship they have with their manager and with other team members. They don't lose all trust per se, but they lose trust that their relationship with you and others is strong enough for them to communicate openly and honestly, and they lose trust that you have their back.

#3 Treating employees like psychopaths

It's been estimated that up to three to four per cent of the population display the characteristics of a psychopath. Psychopaths are willing to consciously lie and manipulate to get their way without a second thought about how their actions impact others. People with psychopathic tendencies can cause untold damage to organisations, and managers would do well protecting themselves from them.

However, as previously discussed, when presented with an employee with a mental health problem, many managers are concerned that they may be being manipulated. The fact that employee mental health problems do tend to emerge more frequently in times of change or organisational stress can provide a context that makes a mental health concern look suspiciously like a tactic to further the employee's interests.

Few managers have the psychiatric training to correctly diagnose psychopathy and, statistically, it is far more likely that the problem is genuine. A smart manager will not have let things progress this far, to the point where there is effectively zero trust between the manager and the employee, making manipulation a consideration.

A good mental health program needs to look at the culture of the organisation, and encourage managers to promote trust and respect in every interaction with employees. Real psychopaths cannot operate in these conditions and will opt out.

#4 Disabling rather than enabling

When managers don't know how to respond to someone experiencing mental distress, a typical response is to try to support the person by removing any potential stressors. They may say 'don't worry about doing that report/job/project—we'll let someone else on the team pick that up', or 'you only need to do half the number of widgets/jobs/activities for now'.

While the intention is good, and this may indeed be helpful in some circumstances, the problem is that in many cases this actually ends up disabling the person. It says that they are not capable of doing the job. And often times the person themselves starts believing it too. Their self esteem declines, they worry that teammates will judge them for not pulling their weight, it can cause conflict, and ultimately the person can experience more distress not less.

As a manager who is looking to build a team of confident, resilience and high performing employees, who feel empowered in their work and life, that's the last thing you want!

#5 Encouraging medication as a first line of treatment

While many people find relief through medication, clinical trials show that it can open a Pandora's box of side effects. Some of these side effects come with more dire consequences than the initial presenting condition. Many managers are not aware of this (and to be fair, it's not explained thoroughly in the glossy brochures).

Some of the more severe proven effects of psychiatric medications include higher suicide risk and risk of violence towards others. This is because they affect the prefrontal cortex of the brain—the part responsible for inhibitions. The prefrontal cortex is the sensible, logical part of the brain—the part that tells you, 'No, it's probably not a good idea to yell at that person right now,' or 'It's not a good idea to hurt myself or to punch my boss.' Just as someone under the influence of alcohol might have their inhibitions lowered, so too does someone under the influence of psychiatric medications. But, of course, this is rarely explained when they're being prescribed. So when the depressed person starts taking antidepressants and then begins to feel worse and have thoughts of suicide, they don't know what is going on. They think it must be them, and they are more likely to act on those thoughts and feelings.

As a manager, can you afford to introduce such levels of unpredictability into your team? Are you really qualified and prepared to make that recommendation? And if one of your team members chooses medication, as is their right, are you ready to monitor them? Monitoring is important for their safety and yours.

The literature contains evidence that ongoing use of psychotropic medication can even slow down the recovery of people with mental health problems, making the mental health problem last longer.

Now, we want to make it very clear right here that we are not anti-medication. We believe it has a role to play, in the right situations. But it is definitely not the first line of treatment. And definitely not something to be forced on someone. People deserve to have the right information so they can make an informed choice about their body and their lives.

Rather than encouraging medication, managers should avoid stepping outside the boundaries of their role, and instead encourage the person to consider a range of options to address their mental health concerns, to get as much information as they can from a range of professionals, and to ask questions so they can make informed choices.

It is never helpful for managers to say, 'If they just took their medication, it would all be fine.' In our experience, and the experience of people who have recovered, medication alone is rarely, if ever, a recipe for recovery. For example, if someone is depressed because of an event that has happened, no amount of medication will change that situation. It might help ease the suffering for a while, but another kind of healing is needed. Managers who resort to medication as the 'cure all' are showing their lack of empathy and their ignorance.

Besides the side effects noted above, medications can have a range of other impacts too. Common ones include nausea, agitation, drowsiness, dizziness, dry mouth, headaches, insomnia, weight gain, flatulence, rashes, mood changes, food cravings, heart problems, body odour, loss of libido, and so on. Not particularly pleasant, and another reason why many people decide it's better to manage the mental health issue in other ways.

#6 Using employee assistance programs and stress leave as the default response

Employee assistance programs (EAP) and personal leave are important tools in your mental health toolbox. However, they are overly relied upon. Both tools, when used too often, send subtle but powerful messages to the broader workforce:

- 'We'll arrange for EAP sessions for anyone with a mental health issue.' *Translation*: 'We don't want to, or know how to, deal with those kind of issues. Go speak to EAP. Please don't involve me because I don't know what to say.'
- 'We will approve leave for people with a mental illness.'

  Translation: 'There's nothing wrong with the workplace; it's all to do with you. Go take some time off and pull yourself together. Then come back when you're ready to work.' And at the same time: 'The workplace is a dangerous place to be, and would not be good for you right now.'

Are these types of messages going to get you the long-term results you want?

#7 Mishandling the performance management process

In practice, probably one of the most sensitive areas managers handle at work is performance management. First, I need to clarify that when we are talking about performance management in this case, we are speaking about the situations in which there is a problem with performance or conduct that needs to be addressed, not the ongoing performance management activities of reviewing and improving the performance of all employees.

Performance management can be a difficult process for everyone involved, regardless of whether there is a mental health issue. The nature of a performance management or other disciplinary processes is that an aspect of your performance or conduct is being scrutinised and judged as not good enough. As humans, we tend to attach our feelings of self-worth and self-esteem to our work. In someone who is already vulnerable, this can be the straw that breaks the camel's back, if that extra stress exceeds their ability to cope.

It is important to remember that in any performance management situation, you can have a couple of different scenarios:

1. **The person may not have any mental health problem, but the process itself precipitates it.** This is probably the rarest scenario. Unless the person is already somewhat vulnerable, or unless the process itself is clearly inappropriate, then it is unlikely that an otherwise healthy person would develop a mental health problem from performance management processes alone.

2. **The person has an underlying mental health problem or vulnerability that they didn't know about, and the performance management process exacerbates it.** This is much more common. While the person might not feel they necessarily had any mental health issue, they may have had a certain amount of stress, or they may have had unhelpful ways of thinking that made them at risk of mental ill health should they be faced with something challenging like a performance management process.

3. **The person may have a mental health problem that they know about, but they have not disclosed it to their employer for fear of it creating problems.** One of the common scenarios we see here is that the process begins, and doesn't go very smoothly, and then halfway through, the person does disclose their mental health diagnosis—usually while explaining that it has been worsened by the performance management process. This, especially, is where things can really start to head downhill very quickly. Typically, managers don't know how to respond in those scenarios and in their attempts to do what they think is right, they can make it all a lot worse. In our courses for managers, we spend a good deal of time looking at

these case scenarios, breaking down what may be going on for the individuals involved, and looking at how they might best respond.

4. **The person has a mental health condition and the manager is aware of this.** In these scenarios, we tend to see a lot of caution on the behalf of the manager. They are usually very concerned that if they say the wrong thing, they could make the mental health of the person worse, or make themselves liable for a bullying or harassment claim against them. And so, managers tend to avoid acting at all. Or if they do, it is to be overly accommodating, which usually means the performance improvement required is not achieved. Either way, not a great outcome for anyone.

Now let me add another layer onto these four scenarios, by telling you that people with a mental health condition, diagnosed or otherwise, are more likely to feel bullied and harassed in general. Whether or not that is actually happening in the interactions, they are more likely to experience performance management in that way—sometimes, no matter how you nicely you couch it. Depending on their sensitivity to it, even regular everyday feedback can feel like criticism and bullying. And the person may be more likely to put in a complaint, in an attempt to right the perceived wrong.

So it can be very tricky to judge:

- **Was there actual bullying and harassment?** In many cases, there was. People with mental health issues often have a strong 'bull*** detector' (excuse the language). And they may be more likely to pick up on more subtle forms of bullying that others wouldn't identify, or would just tolerate.

- **Did it just feel that way to the person?** This is very difficult, as we need to respect the person's experience. Note, even if the final outcome is not as the person wanted, it can still be very important that the person is allowed the opportunity to take the matter further, so as to feel that their objection has been heard, and that they had a right to voice it.
- **Are they deliberately using it as an excuse/counter attack?** Don't assume that everyone with a mental health issue is a nice person. They may be desperate, hurt, angry, or just malicious, like anyone else.

So, as you can see, it can all get pretty messy, pretty quickly. But that doesn't mean it should be avoided. In fact, avoiding the issue entirely is sure to land you in even more trouble! What is most important is the way in which these matters are handled. THAT is what will have the biggest impact on the person. It is vital that managers, and especially Human Resources personnel, have a good understanding of these matters and that all have clear and fair protocols to follow, which are based on good mental health understandings. Sticking to the procedure is the best way to protect everyone in these matters.

Having gone through these common mistakes, it makes sense to turn next to closer consideration of the manager's actual role when it comes to mental health—and what you should, as well as shouldn't, be doing.

4

The Manager's Role

G iven everything we've discussed so far, it's forgivable if you're experiencing some confusion about just what you should be doing. It may seem that we're laying a heap of responsibility on your doorstep, but there's an important boundary when it comes to where that responsibility ends.

What's NOT your job?

An important question to consider before we turn to what you *can* do is: What shouldn't you be expected to do?

Don't be a counsellor

Taking on a counselling role is counterproductive. Doing so blurs the lines of responsibility. It can precipitate you into a position where you take on responsibility for looking after the person, in all aspects, and at the same time, the staff member can lose any sense of personal power as they allow or even expect you, the manager, to 'fix things' for them. You can end up being made to feel responsible for anything that goes wrong and, worse, being held responsible.

Take, for example, a situation we've come across with more than one manager. Let's call our manager here Sarah. Sarah was a very caring and compassionate person, who found out that one of the members on her team had been diagnosed with anxiety and mild depression. Sarah took an active interest in all her staff, and was proud of her ability to develop close bonds with each of them. But in the case of this particular staff member, she started learning more and more about their personal situation, which was very difficult. The staff member would ask her, 'What should I do?' and Sarah would do her best to give her some ideas, but inevitably, it would come back that 'It didn't work,' or 'I've tried that already.' Slowly, bit by bit, the conversations with the staff member became less and less about her work and more and more about her mental health and what the doctor, her counsellor, and her sister had said about it. This continued to the point where the staff member would come in for a forty-minute conversation up to three times a day. She was also coming into work late and not meeting her deadlines, but Sarah felt bad because she knew what this staff member was going through. She couldn't turn her away when she was in need, and she definitely couldn't discipline her through any performance management process. In fact, there were problems with this staff member's car, so Sarah started driving her home each day. Other staff became disgruntled because they were picking up the slack in terms of the work this staff member was not doing, and they felt Sarah was playing favourites. It all went further downhill from there…

So how do you know if you are stepping into the role of counsellor? Each conversation will be different, but there are a few rules of thumb which you can stick to as a starting point:

a. Do not enquire into the person's personal life. Keep any discussion of mental health relevant to the impact on the workplace, and the person's wellbeing at work. The individual themselves may start talking about their personal life, but this doesn't mean they have given you permission to ask questions about it or delve deeper.

b. Do not offer any suggestions about changes the person should make in their personal life. It's okay to discuss options for seeking support and advice, but the manager is not in the position to provide the advice themselves. For example, if the staff member has told you they are experiencing anxiety over financial problems, it would be appropriate to ask if they would consider contacting a financial advice service, but it's definitely not your role to provide financial advice! Or if they discuss problems with their relationship—again, you might ask if they would consider seeking help with that from a professional relationship counsellor, but you wouldn't provide any marital advice yourself.

c. Do not analyse their history and what has led them to their current situation of mental distress. This might be very interesting, but it is just not your role as a manager, and can lead you into dangerous territory which can leave the person at risk, and also leave you at risk.

Don't be a rule maker

Don't create more rules than are absolutely necessary. Many workplaces are heavily burdened by the volume of policies in place, which very few people want or read. More policies, office etiquette or moralising in the workplace won't help you in the battle against mental problems. It will only add to them.

On countless occasions, I've seen managers detract from the quality of their leadership by making an issue out of something that's completely natural for the staff member. For example, one of the things most people need in order to lift themselves out of anxiety or depression is a good dose of anger. Anger is a powerful emotion and very useful as a change agent. Much better than despair! Most people can think of a time when a good, emotionally-charged swearword helped them get over a hurdle, right? But what do poor leaders do? They try to regulate against anger at all times. It may show up in the form of prohibiting swearing, or putting in place other policies as to the 'right way' to behave, etc. I'm not saying here that we should all swear like sailors, or that we should have punch-ups in the office. Anger needs to be expressed appropriately. What I'm saying is that we shouldn't be so precious that natural emotions are squashed before they are expressed fully and in a constructive way. It's important for people to have a certain degree of freedom if they are to do well mentally.

A note on swearing: A study where participants were made to keep their hands submerged in cold water, and asked to rate the amount of pain they felt, found that swearing actually reduced the amount of pain felt. Participants were able to keep their hands in the cold water longer and reported experiencing less pain when they repeated a swearword in contrast to when they repeated another word. In other words, swearing made them more resilient. While we don't condone swearing as a regular practice, and certainly don't approve of its use in settings with customers, we caution against removing it as a coping mechanism for people in particularly stressful situations. It's not the biggest issue on the table here.

Don't make a diagnosis

This is not your role, and neither are you qualified to do it. What would be the point of it, anyway? Let's say that you diagnose a team member with Generalised Anxiety Disorder. Now what? Where do you go from here? You may feel very smart and proud of yourself. You may even feel vindicated. After all, your team would be perfect if it wasn't for that particularly annoying staff member that... do you see where I'm going with this?

Even the mental health field is plagued by problems that come from diagnosing people. There is evidence to show that a person's recovery takes an additional five years if there's a diagnosis. Why? Basic human nature. People are naturally inclined to follow social proof.

In one study, researchers sent substitute teachers to a school. Some were told their class was the worst performing class when the opposite was true—their class was the best performing class in the school. Within a short time, the class was underperforming and had behavioural problems. The perception of the teacher, the leader, coloured and informed the results obtained. Other substitute teachers were sent to the worst class but told they were the best performing students. Do you want to guess what happened? They ended up being very good students. What do we learn from this? That the perception and attitude of the leader influences the identity of the followers. Can you now see what could happen if you took it upon yourself to identify people with a diagnosis?

Don't solve an employee's mental health problem

If it's not your problem, don't make it yours. If you do, you will become the proud, or distressed, owner of a brand new problem, but you won't have any power whatsoever to solve it. Why? Because it's not yours. And people resent others trying to take their problems away from them.

They'll fight you for the right to have that problem. Ever tried giving advice that hasn't been requested?

So the above has outlined some lines not to cross, but what *can* you do? What's within the healthy boundaries of your role? What are your opportunities to effect change in this difficult area?

Who is driving the bus?

Remember when we talked about the commando team in the introduction? If you read the description thinking, 'That doesn't sound at all like my team,' you're not alone. It means there is an opportunity here to reflect on how things got to be the way they are and what you can do about it. One of the things that can help is to ask yourself: Who is driving the bus?

There are a couple of different buses we are talking about. The first is the 'team bus'. So the question is: Who is really leading your team?

Is it you? Or are there one or more informal influencers who seem to be subverting or redirecting others on the team? When you introduce a new project, a new idea, or a new way of working, how does the team respond? Does the change happen? Or do people nod in agreement yet change nothing? There is always someone leading the team. If it's not you, then it must be someone else. And that is not a good position to be in as a leader. You want to be the one driving the bus.

When it comes to managing workplace mental health effectively, we know that for the team to have good mental health, they need a strong leader. They need someone who can stand up to the first whiff of stigma or discrimination. They need someone who is willing to address the sensitive topics, and do so from a place of certainty, empowerment and leadership.

Of course, that doesn't mean you always have to have a top down, directive approach—there can be room for discussion and collaboration and input from all, but at the end of the day, you have been placed in a leadership position for one purpose—to LEAD the team.

The second bus is your 'internal bus'—your mind, if you like. Who is in charge of you?

Do you lead your mind and use it to get where you want to go, or does it lead you? If you want to lead a team effectively to positive mental health, you'll need to be in charge of your own internal bus. The fact that mental health problems are so widespread means that it is likely you yourself might have experienced your own mental health challenges, or know someone—a friend or family member—who has. And there may be some sensitive topics for you individually. You need to be aware of that and manage yourself through it, keeping those previous experiences separate from what might be going on with a team member.

The very nature of mental health issues means the issue is so personal for the person experiencing it that they may want to make it personal for you, too. You need to be driving your own bus, so you can stay calm and in control if that happens.

Emotional intelligence in the workplace

Daniel Goleman is responsible for bringing the concept of 'emotional intelligence' to the public's attention. In basic terms, he draws the distinction between emotional intelligence (EQ) and intellectual intelligence (IQ). In his book, he outlines five areas of emotional intelligence, and explains that leaders who are strong in these emotional skills are more likely to experience great results in many areas of life, including their careers. While technical skills and knowledge (IQ) may be required to enter an industry or a specific job role, the ability to manage yourself (EQ) is what makes you shine in that role and gets you promoted.

We would add to that that in order to effectively manage mental health in the workplace, these skills are vital. It's not just about following a certain process (though that can be important too). To really manage others well, you'll need to draw on your emotional intelligence.

The question 'who is driving the bus?' is a starting point for reflecting on these five areas of emotional intelligence: self-awareness, self-regulation, motivation, empathy and social skills.

Self-awareness: To effectively manage mental health in the workplace, the leaders must be aware of their own mental health and wellbeing. They must be able to identify when they are having a day which sees them slightly lower on the mental health continuum than they would normally be. They must be able to identify their own filter for mental health, and recognise that their own life experiences might be impacting how they view a certain situation with a staff member.

Self-regulation: Once the leader is self-aware in relation to mental health, they need to be able to control their responses to others. If they are having an 'off day', they need to be able to ensure that this does not impact the wellbeing of their team members. They should hold themselves to a higher standard than anyone else. After all, staff are looking to their leaders as a model for how to behave at work.

Motivation: To address mental health and wellbeing in the workplace, the leaders must have a good, strong 'why' to motivate them towards improving the wellbeing of their team. That 'why' is the reason, the rationale, the drive that allows them to persist in leading a happy, healthy and high-performing team, even in the face of some of the obstacles we have already discussed in terms of workplace mental health.

Empathy: Clearly, when addressing mental health issues on an individual basis with particular staff members, the EI skill of having empathy is invaluable. This is different to 'sympathy', which can be described as feeling 'sorry for' a person. Rather, empathy is about diving into the other person's shoes, and doing your best to experience their feelings. Of course, you'll never know exactly what it is like for them to experience mental distress, as it is so unique to the individual. But this skill is about respecting and acknowledging their experience as a human being. One human to another.

Social skills: Finally, this element of EI comes down to the ability to communicate effectively with the person in distress. In our Mental Health Masterclass for Leaders, we explore a framework for having conversations with the person about mental health. A good, solid foundation in social skills—being able to respond effectively, both verbally and nonverbally—forms the basis of a mental health conversation that will go well.

Now we've looked at what you can do on a personal level to take control of your bus and improve your emotional intelligence, let's look at what you can achieve in the workplace.

PART TWO

The 7 Pillars of a Mentally Wealthy Workplace

What is Mental Wealth?

Workplace mental wealth describes the business potential of an organisation in terms of being the direct result of how well the organisation fosters the mental health of its people.

It's a measure of your organisation's ability to create, collaborate, problem-solve and take initiative. It's a measure of your team's resilience and ability to keep going when things are tough and uncertain. These 'soft' factors are more important these days than ever. It's the passion, creativity and collaborative efforts of an organisation's people that create wealth for shareholders.

This is why we use the term 'mental wealth' to highlight the importance of mental health for the wealth of the company. We're talking in financial terms, of course, but also in terms of emotional wealth.

Mentally wealthy workplaces display the following characteristics:

- People are focused, creative and highly productive, and free of debilitating chronic stress and anxiety.
- The dynamic between people in an organisation is one of respect and inclusion, where people feel free to voice opinions and contribute ideas, for which they are valued as an employee and as a person.
- Leaders truly recognise the value of people, and encourage diversity in values and styles. They actively curtail behaviours that diminish or demean others.
- There is a positive organisational climate, absent of bullying and harassment, mental injury and stress claims, and mental health crises.

To define and, therefore, help managers build mental wealth in their organisations, we have developed the 7 Pillars of a Mentally Wealthy Workplace. These pillars were created to answer the question: 'What does a mentally healthy workplace look like?' They have been derived from looking around the world at what is recognised as best practice when assisting people with severe mental health issues to recover. We've then translated them for and applied them to a workplace context. This is not with the aim of helping people to recover from their mental health problem, necessarily, but with the aim of ensuring that workplaces are as psychologically safe and healthy environments as possible for all people, regardless of where they fall on the mental health scale at any particular point in time.

These seven pillars can be applied at the individual level, in terms of the one-on-one relationship and conversations had between a manager and a team member. They can also be applied at the organisational level in terms of the development of your Workplace Mental Health and Wellbeing Strategy. We'll explain how in each pillar.

The seven pillars work best when applied together, but even the commitment to adopt and implement just one of these pillars will make a massive difference in your workplace. If you work towards adopting all of them, you'll be setting up a workplace culture that is best practice when it comes to workplace mental health.

Let's explore each pillar in detail.

Pillar 1

We Not You

Mentally healthy workplaces think in terms of 'we' not 'you'. This means that the focus is not on *'those'* individuals with a mental health problem, but on the health and wellbeing of all employees, managers included. It recognises that mental health problems can affect anyone, and that we will all go through challenges in life and work at one time or another. At the individual level, the question is not: 'What do YOU need to do to get better?' or 'What do YOU need to do to perform?' It's: 'What can WE do, together, to be healthy and to perform?' At the organisational level, it is not about creating policies and procedures to deal with those people who become unwell; it's about creating policies and procedures that work for any of us, should WE become unwell or need assistance at any point in time—regardless of our position in the hierarchy.

Using' 'us' and 'them' language can be a sign of stigma existing within the organisation. Rather than a culture characterised by stigma, a mentally wealthy workplace has a culture that displays *unconditional positive regard.*

Unconditional positive regard

In today's workplaces, research shows that people are afraid to come out and tell their managers they are experiencing mental distress. Why? Because they feel it will hurt their careers or their relationships in the workplace. They believe they will be stigmatised for having a mental health problem. This reflects a deep-seated mistrust between managers and staff. But what if we could effect a paradigm shift in this thinking—a shift in perspective that helps turn the problem into a competitive advantage? We can do this by promoting **unconditional positive regard**.

Unconditional positive regard is a term from psychology which refers to the positive feelings of the counsellor or therapist towards the person seeking help. It describes a position where the help provider has an unwavering respect and appreciation for the person opposite them as a good and worthy human being, regardless of that person's particular behaviours or demeanour. It is the complete belief that this person is good, even if they have done bad things. Parents apply this principle when then demonstrate unconditional love for their child, despite whatever bad behaviour the child has gotten up to. It's the difference between saying, 'You're a bad boy,' versus, 'You're a good boy who did a bad thing.' They may not always be nice, or right, but we can still respect the person. It is an authentic respect for the humanity of the person.

Have you noticed that when you work with people on a daily basis, you have a certain view of them, based on your experiences with them in that context? And then have you ever had the experience where you see the person out of that context? Maybe you bump into them on the weekend somewhere, or you witness their children meeting them at work for whatever reason. Whatever it is, it gives you a sudden and new appreciation of the person as a whole person, not just the part you see in a working context. If we can remember the humanity of each person, we will go a long way to feeling and then showing that unconditional positive regard for them.

In an organisation demonstrating unconditional positive regard, people are convinced that managers value and appreciate them as contributing members despite their mental health challenges and, at times, even *because of those challenges*. Now, that sounds counterintuitive doesn't it? Let me explain with a story.

The canary in the coal mine

In days gone by, miners would take a small canary down into the coal mine with them. Coal mining was a much more dangerous profession than it is today, and one of the silent killers was toxic and highly flammable gases. These gases were often odourless, so the miners wouldn't know they were ingesting them until they lost consciousness or a spark caused an explosion and cave-in. Because the canary was a more sensitive animal, it would start showing symptoms of toxic gas poisoning before the miners. So the miners would keep an eye on the canary and if it started looking unwell, what do you think they did?

Well, I can tell you what they didn't do. They didn't say:

- 'Don't worry about it. He's faking it! I'm sure he's faking it.'
- 'He's not pulling his weight, is he?'
- 'I am so busy. I don't have time for this!'

No, *they got the h*** out of the mine.*

They stopped the source of the toxic fumes, and they cleaned up the environment before heading back in.

The miners took care of their canary. They understood that the canary had a more sensitive nature and that sensitivity was an asset to the team. In our organisations, we should be adopting the same approach. We should ask ourselves: What 'toxic fumes' could be present in this team / culture / organisation that no one else seems to have sensed yet, but that everybody is breathing?

Just as the canary has a particular nature which was more sensitive—more attuned to any toxic fumes—the person with a mental health problem can be the one who is calling out the problems which are lying undetected, which will sooner or later affect others on the team too. In fact, it's likely that if there is one canary on your team who is calling out any problems, there are also others who are having the same issues, but who have not yet said anything.

So, as managers, we should ask ourselves: *What 'toxic fumes' could be present in this team that no one else seems to have sensed yet, but that everybody is breathing?*

We can go searching for the answers to that question ourselves, or we can ask the canary—in a sense, treating them as a consultant. They can take the temperature of the team.

This might sound completely unrealistic, especially if you've had challenges before managing someone experiencing mental distress—after all, they often become the 'problem person', don't they? But it doesn't have to be that way. Often, by treating the person with genuine respect and dignity, and accepting them for their unique qualities, you can get a better outcome in the long run.

This approach is, in essence, a 'strengths-based' approach. You might have heard that term before, or at least the philosophy that you should focus on people's strengths. But we see that, often, managers pay lip service to the idea, while not truly valuing the diverse strengths of their team members. In this pillar, we are challenging you, as a manager, to stretch yourself here. To truly start to see the strengths of each team member, even in their apparent weaknesses.

There are no victims

In recognising the strengths the person brings to the team, we must also remember to treat the person as a fully capable and competent person. Just because they are experiencing some challenges at the moment, it does not make them a poor, vulnerable 'victim'.

One of the problems we see in workplaces is that many managers are empathetic to the struggles that their team member is going through, but so much so that they begin to treat the person like a 'victim'— helpless to do anything for themselves. Though it's not their intention, when this happens, the manager often ends up spending an exorbitant amount of time on that one individual staff member (at the expense of other team members or projects); they may provide more leniencies than they normally would on work projects, which, of course, doesn't go down well with other team members; and they can start to cross the boundaries of their role, becoming entwined in the person's personal situation, giving personal advice or staying after hours to help, etc. Remember Sarah's story? Basically, they step into the role of 'hero' to the so-called 'victim'.

Again, it's not the intention of the manager, but when someone begins to treat the person like a victim by over-helping, they unconsciously send the message to the person that they are not able to do it on their own—that they need others to do the basics. And it creates a self-fulfilling prophecy. As a manager who wants to build a team of 'commandos', this is not a good place to be.

Ultimately, what happens is that the manager themselves often ends up becoming frustrated when all their well-intentioned advice gets ignored, when they are lying awake at night worrying about the person, and when it seems like the person is not doing anything for themselves. The manager then moves into the role of 'villain', likely to express their frustration with the person, giving them a 'piece of their mind'. It's a desperate attempt to get the person to help themselves, but it leaves the 'victim' feeling even more distressed—and even more justified in their victim state. After all, their manager was supposed to help them, but now they're attacking them. Many a manager has fallen for this trap and ended up in trouble themselves for saying something they shouldn't have.

Of course, no one intends for this to happen. The person with mental distress was not consciously manipulating the situation. The manager started out wanting to help. But we've seen it happen too many times.

Adopting an 'us' not 'you' stance, remembering the canary in the coal mine, helps the manager to remember the strengths of the individual and to treat them with both respect and compassion.

The toxic fume: Otherness

Using the analogy of the mines, we have identified a toxic fume underlying each pillar. For this pillar, the toxic fume is **'otherness'**— that separation of yourself from others who might be unwell or more sensitive to becoming unwell.

'We Not You' is about acknowledging that we are all in this together. It's about thinking, 'Hang on. One of our members is not well. That member is actually expressing what quite a few members in the team are not expressing, or perhaps haven't noticed yet. Let's fix the problem before the rest of us go down with the same symptoms.'

It's not *your* problem, but OUR problem, OUR opportunity.

How do you apply this pillar?

In one-on-one conversations and interactions with colleagues, it can be as simple as using language of 'we' and 'us', as opposed to 'you' and 'them'.

Let me give you an example. Imagine you are sitting in a meeting with your superior. Perhaps you've raised a concern about something. Your manager could respond in a myriad of ways, but just for fun, let's listen to the difference in these two responses:

- 'How can you fix this?'
- 'How can we fix this?'

What do you notice?

If your manager says, 'How can you fix this?' it's likely you feel that your concern has not really been heard, or that they don't really care, or don't want to take any responsibility for it. It has simply been swatted back to you, like a ping pong ball.

Now, compare that to: 'How can we fix this?' Doesn't that immediately sound better? Doesn't it suddenly feel like the manager is acknowledging and immediately accepting the concern you've raised? It suggests that they are genuinely looking for a way for you both to address this together. Now the problem solving process can begin. You are both looking for a way to resolve the problem, or at least resolve your concerns about it. This demonstrates an approach of curiosity and collaboration. It also means that, as a manager, you don't have to have all the answers. In fact, the person who spotted the problem is likely to be way ahead of you in considering various responses, in thinking about what is needed.

At an organisational level, adopting the 'We Not You' pillar could mean the creation of a Workplace Mental Health and Wellbeing Strategy that clearly applies to all employees. That would be demonstrated in the language used, but it would also recognise that ALL employees have a responsibility to care for their mental health, and it would state a commitment to supporting staff wherever they may be on the mental health continuum.

> **Mentally healthy workplaces think in terms of 'us' not 'you'. Rather than a culture characterised by stigma, theirs displays unconditional positive regard. Acknowledging mutual responsibility, a culture of blame is replaced by one of shared concern.**

Initiatives

The following is a list of initiatives you could implement to support this pillar:

- Hold a mental health awareness session to introduce your organisation's commitment to look after the mental health and wellbeing of all employees. It can include some basic information about mental health and things all people can do to stay well.

- Train your staff in basic mental health skills. For example, implement our one-day Mental Health Essentials workshop, which teaches participants how to identify the common mental health issues which may present in a workplace setting, and how to respond to a colleague who may be experiencing mental distress. It also covers what to do in a mental health emergency situation. (www.wmhi.com.au/mental-health-essentials/)

- Display some posters promoting good mental health and a compassionate attitude. You can download ours at: https://www.wmhi.com.au/mental-health-awareness-posters/

- Put an article about mental wellness in the newsletter each week/month. This could be a story about someone who has recovered, information about a local service, or an upcoming community event.

- Publish workplace mental health posts on social media. Keep them light and positive.

- Invite guest speakers with lived experience to talk to groups. It's important to choose your speakers carefully. They should be someone who has fully recovered who can show that it is possible, and who has a very positive attitude towards life.

- Start an internal online forum, such as a closed Facebook group or intranet forum, with resources about different mental health issues, and other things that affect mental health and wellbeing like sleep, diet, physical activity, and so on.

- Ask people in leadership positions if they have a story of recovery from mental distress they are willing to share (for example, as an interview in a newsletter). This sends a very strong message that it's okay to talk about mental health, and that there are individuals in senior positions in the organisation who know what the challenges can be. Again, it is important the person has fully recovered, has a balanced perspective, and is ready for their personal story to be public. But if it is done well, it can create a lot of trust.

- Educate all staff on mental health as part of their induction training. A number of organisations we work with have incorporated a module on mental health and wellbeing into their induction program, alongside their Occupational Health

& Safety training. This helps to create a healthy culture from the outset.

Pillar 2

Organisational Plasticity

This pillar is about embracing **organisational plasticity**. This is a key trait of mentally wealthy workplaces, where *authentic flexibility replaces fear and rigidity.*

The world is changing, if you hadn't noticed! We are no longer in the industrial age of factories, where people were viewed in terms of machines, and judged simply on their ability to produce. The modern workplace recognises the benefits of a diverse workforce, where each employee brings their unique blend of skills, talents and background to the job at hand. No longer is the employee expected to fulfil the role of a machine in exactly the same way the next person would. Instead, employees are expected to think, problem-solve, show initiative, and so on. But in return for these demands, and when recruiting a diverse workforce, we must be willing to cater to the different and unique needs and styles of those employees. We need to be flexible to accommodate and get the best out of different people.

Take the authors as an example. Emi loves structure: a room, a computer, a desk, somewhere to focus and crank stuff out. But for Peter, just talking about it... ugh. Give him a laptop on the beach, or in a coffee shop, and then his mind starts flowing. For Peter, putting someone at a desk and asking them to sit there for eight hours a day—surely that would be torture! To him, it seems dull and lacking in creativity. Whereas to someone like Emi, wanting to take a laptop to the beach looks like a lack of commitment, or some sort of ADHD thing.

The problem is, in many workplaces, we don't truly appreciate the diversity in working styles and we are too quick to judge. So we decide that we had better put some controls in place to make sure that others work and act how we think they should. That control rankles and it forces the person to perform from a position of weakness, not in a way that amplifies their talents. This is where we need to examine ourselves and say, 'Are we unfairly judging someone because they are different?'

Flexibility with filters

One way to offer flexibility is to apply the concept of filters, which we explored in Part 1 of this book. A 'filter' is a specific way that a person makes sense of their world and their life. When it comes to workplace mental health, this means that different individuals will have different understandings of what mental health and wellbeing is, and what is needed to help them be well at work. Precisely the things that work for one person may be the opposite of what is needed for someone else.

Speaking specifically about mental health for now, our society currently favours the 'medical' and 'psychological' filters for mental health and wellbeing. This is why, when someone is unwell, most workplaces encourage the person to seek medical help, or counselling (usually through an Employee Assistance Program). But as you now know, not everyone views mental health through these lenses. And forcing someone to seek help through your filter instead of their own may not only fail to work, but actually make things worse. It can lead to conflict, resistance and, in some cases, complaints of harassment and/ or bullying.

As a case in point, for many years, when there was some kind of critical or traumatic incident, it was thought that the best way to help people was to get everyone together and hold a 'mandatory debriefing' so that everyone could talk about what had happened, and how they felt about it. What was discovered, though, was that for people who don't process things well that way, being forced to focus on what had happened, and relive it over and over, actually made things worse. These people were being re-traumatised during that debriefing. That is why it is now recommended that workplaces *offer* debriefing and support to any employees who want it, but *don't force* people to attend a mandatory debriefing.

What we still see happening in workplaces is having these two avenues of support—the doctor and EAP. Those people who hold a different filter as their predominant model of the world just don't access that support, because they don't think it will help them. And if it's just not their filter, they are right! We know that for people to address their mental distress, they are much more likely to access help through their existing filter before trying a new one, and much more likely to recover through their own filter.

Organisations need to have a range of different options that appeal to people who use different filters.

Flexibility of working conditions

Let me give you another example of how organisational plasticity can be applied. This one comes up a lot in our training courses and consulting. It is often recommended that in order to have a good 'work-life balance', people should set timeframes for their working hours—let's use Monday to Friday 9 to 5pm as an easy example—and outside of those hours, they should not engage in, talk about or even think about anything to do with their work.

Firstly, we question how doable this really is—especially at the higher levels of an organisation, where you tend to find the people who are more actively progressing their careers. In order to get ahead, working after hours might be required—whether it's the CEO reading up on the latest market trends on his Sunday morning, a C Suite executive finishing up some loose ends before they head home for the day, or the mid level manager doing some professional development or a home study course after hours. When it comes to all employees, can we really expect people not to think about something work-related after work?

Second, what does this say about work anyway? It implies that work is a bad place to be—if you're there too much or you do too much, you'll get sick. Ideally, it should be a nice and positive environment to be in, and we should recognise that people can have a passion for whatever it is they do.

It is true that balance is important, and it's not a good idea for people to ruminate and stress about work all the time, but it's also not useful to force people into specific styles of working that don't match their style—where they then feel guilty for having a work-related thought!

That C suite executive, for example, may find themselves more stressed due to leaving their desk at 5pm, with unfinished tasks, than they would if they stayed an extra twenty minutes to finish them off in the peace and quiet of a deserted office. Of course, if they're staying till 2am on a regular basis, to the detriment of their health and family life, then perhaps it's something to look at. But who makes the call as to what is the right balance for that person? Our answer is simple—it's that person! That individual has the right to make the call as to what works for them.

Some people are 9 to 5 people, some people are early risers and work best 6am to 3pm, and some work well in the night-time. As a workplace, can you accommodate individuals' own preferences, provided the work gets done? Obviously, in some workplaces, that level of flexibility is not possible for business reasons (for example, in nursing or other occupations where there is a requirement for a certain level of staffing at certain times). And there are other considerations to take into account as well. But what's more important is to ask the question: 'Where *can* we be flexible to support the differing needs of our employees?'

This same principle of organisational flexibility can apply in a range of areas, such as location of work (e.g. office, on site, at home,) and use of workspace (e.g., desk, employee lounge, outside areas), for example.

Getting the balance right

When it comes to dealing with people who are experiencing mental distress, many managers feel way out of their depth. There is a lot of uncertainty and insecurity about what needs to be done. Managers want to make sure they do the right thing, and fear the repercussions if the situation goes pear shaped. As a result, this fear leads many managers to close off to the person, rather than opening up. Managers often fear that they will be taken advantage of, or that they will make a mistake that will hurt their reputation. This can lead managers to lean too far towards the side of rigidity, control and micro-management.

In the previous pillar, we warned against treating the person with a mental health issue like a 'victim'. But on the flip side, we also don't want to go too far the other way. Managers who do are not necessarily bad or unfeeling people; it's just that, often, they've been burnt before, and are hesitant to repeat the experience, so they opt for a hard line approach. 'This is what's going to happen,' 'This is what you need to do,' 'This is the way it's going to be.' As one manager put it, the message to the individual can be: 'Take a spoonful of cement, and harden up!'

Just as the overly accommodating 'rescue' approach can be harmful, so too can the overly rigid and inflexible approach.

The key word here is 'balance'. How do you get the balance right? When we talk about organisational plasticity, we are talking about a balanced approach. Offering flexibility where possible doesn't mean that 'anything goes'. Flexibility has to be provided in a way that supports the business goals as well as the individual.

A good example is in 'flexible adjustments'. In having a conversation with an employee with a mental health problem, for example, we might ask, 'What things do you think we could do to support you right now?' The employee may respond with something outlandish: 'An all expenses paid trip to Fiji would be just the thing to help my recovery.' Of course, you don't have to agree to whatever their suggestion is! But asking the question is still a good idea. From there, you could follow up by saying, 'That's not possible, but what we would like to do is create a 'green room' here on site, where any staff who need a fifteen-minute time out can go, to take a breather or get a cup of tea, before returning to work'. That is flexibility. That is organisational plasticity.

Toxic fume: Fear of making a mistake

In keeping with our canary in the coalmine analogy, one of the toxic fumes that can creep into our teams is the **fear of making a mistake**.

This pillar is probably the one which managers find the most difficult to get their head around. It requires us to celebrate change and uncertainty. It requires the ability to adjust and adapt, to let go of old ways and embrace new ways. It sometimes means we have to trust in our employees not to take advantage of the flexibilities we have offered, and trust in our hiring decisions and the workplace culture we have created.

Managers, these days, can be forgiven for trying to avoid risks at all costs. Often, the consequences of getting it wrong can appear a lesser evil than coping with the symptoms. If they are to take action, they want to follow a definite process—one that will deliver a definite result. But the problem, when it comes to mental health and wellbeing, is that everyone is different. Often, there is no one specific process that will magically 'work' for everyone. What there can be is a set of principles that can be applied.

This toxic fume leads to more policies, rules, and restrictions. Unfortunately, these ever increasing policies tend to adopt a one-size-fits-all approach, which does not support diversity. Organisations need to be open and able to change rapidly to accommodate new ways of thinking—including new ways of thinking about mental health.

How do you apply this pillar?

At the individual level, this pillar is about treating each person as unique, while having fair processes in place for the team.

Managers can apply this pillar by becoming aware of their own filter for mental health. When you know your preferred filter, you know your bias. Then, you can be careful not to push this onto your employees. Instead, get to know the individual employees who report to you. Learn what their filters are and what works for them to feel good at work. You don't have to read their mind—it can be as simple as asking them.

Ask yourself and your team, 'In our industry and workplace, how can we be more flexible and better accommodate the needs of our employees?'

Spend some time reflecting on your own management style. Do you tend towards being overly sympathetic to people experiencing mental distress, which can be disempowering for you and for them? Or do you tend to take an overly rigid and tough approach without providing any flexibility for people with different needs? Or do you have the balance right?

At the organisational level, as a workplace, do you have a range of avenues for support that cover different filters? For example, for people with a spiritual filter, is there a non-denominational chaplain whom people can access if needed? For people with a trauma filter, do you have information about various support groups in the community who can assist? For people with a 'diet and exercise' filter, can you provide details of a good nutritionist? Do you have subsidised gym memberships? And what about Chinese medicine? As you explore the different filters, you start to expand the range of options which you can offer to your employees, so they can select the things that will start to help them soonest.

Remember that, in Pillar 1: We Not You, we discussed the importance of implementing initiatives that apply for everyone—not just the people who happen to be experiencing a mental health problem right now. In Pillar 2, when we are looking for opportunities to make flexible arrangements, we should ask ourselves, 'Can we offer this to everyone?' Don't just consider those who happen to be experiencing mental distress right now. For example, if we are able to provide a flexible start time (say, anytime between 8am to 10am, so long as you do the minimum eight hours), then maybe we can make this a policy for all staff. Of course, what is possible in terms of reasonable adjustments may differ according to role requirements, but it's the approach of looking for opportunities which works.

Applying this pillar requires organisations and the managers in them to become much more flexible in their thinking. It requires education so that managers understand the concept of filters, diversity, and know how to set these things up in the right way.

Organisational plasticity is a key trait of mentally wealthy workplaces, where authentic flexibility replaces fear and rigidity.

Initiatives

The following is a list of initiatives you could implement to support this pillar:

- Offer two hours each week to every employee to spend on any professional development or work project they are interested in. The well known example of this is Google's twenty per cent time, where, in addition to their regular projects, employees can spend twenty per cent of their time on a project of their choice to benefit Google. They report that many significant advances have come out of the twenty per cent time. There is some speculation about whether it still exists, but, nevertheless, the principle remains. This allows people to work to their natural and individual strengths and talents.

- Implement or extend Employee Assistance Programs (EAP), but also offer subsidised access to a self-selected psychologist, external coaching, and other professionals from across the mental health filters. Make sure to approve the time off for these appointments.

- Offer flexible start and finish times, as explained in this chapter.

- Offer flexibility with days off, for example, two half days instead of full days.

- Provide opportunities for job rotation.

- Provide the opportunity to work from home at least one day a week.

- Offer an allotted number of mental health days (paid or unpaid) for all staff, with no reason required. Of course, if you have a good relationship with your employees, you would hope they feel comfortable enough to talk to you about what is going on. But not everyone will. While there still exists a lot of stigma, don't force people to tell you about their problems. Allow them their privacy and allow them to save face while they do something to look after themselves.

- Make it acceptable to text in sick (phone call not needed) with a code (e.g. green means I'll be okay; amber means check on me; red means get me help). Many workplaces stipulate that if someone is calling in sick, they have to call. This made sense in a time before text messaging was available. But now that there exists another option, by stipulating that it must be a call, we are unconsciously sending the message: 'I don't trust you. You could be faking it. I need to hear your voice to tell if it's the truth or not.' When it comes to a mental health issue, it's not necessarily going to sound like they're sick, anyway. Plus, it is a highly sensitive reason to need time off. Again, let the person save face. If you do decide to accept text as a form of communication, it's a good idea to make it clear policy that they must receive a written response confirming receipt of that message. The code system takes it a step further. If the person texts 'green', no action is necessary. If it's amber, it might mean the manager calling them to check in, or contacting a next of kin. Red means contact the next of kin immediately and let them know it's urgent.

- Introduce casual Fridays. Some people work better when in their comfortable casuals.

Pillar 3

Nothing About Me Without Me

Mentally wealthy workplaces practice **dignified inclusion** rather than secrecy. We call this the principle of 'Nothing About Me Without Me'.

This phrase actually comes from people with a lived experience of mental illness. Many people who have recovered from severe mental ill-health have said that one of the things that made their recovery so difficult was the so-called professionals and 'helpers' who made decisions about their life without their involvement.

Some of the common decisions that people with mental health problems have made for them by others are things like when they will be hospitalised and released, what medication and how much of it they will take, and what they are capable of doing or not. For more severe mental health problems, this can extend to all aspects of life, such as where they will live, whom they can associate with, what they can and can't eat, what time they must go to sleep and wake up, what they should wear, and more. So it's little wonder that many people who have made it through the mental health problem and the system call themselves 'psychiatric survivors', meaning not that they survived the condition, but that they survived the psychiatric system.

Obviously, when you remove a person's ability to make decisions for themselves, they become more and more disempowered, and more and more incapable of making those decisions for themselves in the future. This is the complete opposite of what we are trying to achieve when it comes to recovery from mental distress. We want to help people feel stronger and more confident in themselves.

Unfortunately, while it has been proven that the traditional, top-down approach to managing people with mental health issues does not get the best results, nonetheless, it is still practised in the majority of mental health institutions in Western countries. In the authors' opinion, this is one of the main reasons why mental disorders are treated so poorly.

'Nothing about me without me' was born as a catchcry from people who have recovered, to remind people that even though the person with a mental health problem might have some challenges in thinking clearly or making decisions, they still have the right to be included in decision-making that affects their quality of life. This pillar is about respecting the dignity of the person, and including them, rather than creating secrecy and distrust.

Mentally wealthy workplaces practice dignified inclusion rather than secrecy. We call this the principle of 'Nothing About Me Without Me'

Toxic fume: Distrust

Translated for a workplace context, one of the first things, if not *the* first thing, that suffers when people become distressed and mentally unwell is real trust in the relationship they have with their boss and with other team members. They don't lose all trust, but they lose trust that their relationship with you and others is strong enough for them to communicate openly and honestly; and they lose trust that you really have their back. As this gets worse, it can develop into full-blown paranoia. 'The boss has the door shut... they must be talking about me... I know I didn't do so well on that last project... but they haven't said anything, so they must be planning to get rid of me...' Before you know it, the person is in a complete panic about being fired.

But this distrust can also go two ways. One of the biggest questions managers ask us is: 'How can we tell if someone *really* has a mental illness, or if they are just manipulating me to get some kind of leniency or benefit?' We spoke about this in Part 1, so I won't go into that discussion again, other than to point out that trust and distrust go both ways here.

What happens when the manager doesn't trust the employee, or their own ability to manage workplace mental health, is that they tend to close up. They are likely to speak to everyone else BUT the person themselves, in an attempt to figure out what to do.

This was clearly demonstrated in one organisation we consulted with. When we arrived, we were told a story about Paul. Paul had a fairly good relationship with his manager Beth. One day, when they were talking about a news item that had been on TV the night before, Paul mentioned to Beth, 'Actually, I was diagnosed with bipolar disorder a little while ago.' Beth was very surprised, and didn't quite know how to respond, so she basically dismissed the comment with, 'Oh, really?' and moved onto something else quickly. After she left the conversation with Paul, she went into a panic. What did this mean? What should she do? What if Paul had an episode here at work? What if he was a risk to people? What if he was depressed—how could she support him? Was there some form that should be completed? What was the procedure here?

Completely unsure of what to do or say, she went to her manager and explained the situation. Unfortunately, Beth's manager was equally in the dark. So she went to the HR team, who spoke to Legal, who said they needed to involve the Workplace Health & Safety representative from that department... Anyway, long story short, they decided that in order to best support Paul, someone had better check in on him on a weekly basis, to make sure he was coping okay. And in order to make sure that Paul didn't accuse them of bullying or anything like that (there's that distrust!), there had better be more than one person there for that check-in. Before you knew it, Paul was being pulled into a weekly panel meeting with three of his superiors to ask if he was okay and see if they could offer any support.

Paul hadn't mentioned his diagnosis to anyone else at the office, so no one else knew what was going on. All they saw was that every Thursday, Paul went off to HR for a very serious looking meeting. The rumours started flying that he was being performance managed and could be on his way out of the organisation. Paul heard them and started to wonder if it was true. Meanwhile, he was feeling embarrassed and annoyed at these weekly intrusions into his state of mind. He wished he hadn't said anything to his boss. In fact, this whole situation was now starting to affect his sense of wellbeing, making him feel worse! Come to think of it, having to go through this on the basis of having a diagnosis of mental ill health was starting to feel very discriminatory. After all, his performance was fine before and still was!

All of this could have been avoided by applying the third pillar: 'Nothing About Me Without Me'. In short, no conversation is to take place, and no decisions are to be made, without including the person whom they're about. The person who will be affected . Imagine, instead, in this scenario, that as soon as a discussion started about a person, they were immediately brought into the conversation: *'Hang on, let's get Paul involved, and see what his view is.'* I guarantee you the conversation will be a lot more respectful and productive, and the process will strengthen trust within the team.

Had Beth, or even her manager, just spoken directly with Paul, and asked him, 'Is there anything we need to know, or anything we can do here to support you with that?' it would have opened up a dialogue with Paul, increasing trust instead of decreasing it. Even if Beth were to say, 'You know, Paul, I'm not sure what our organisation's policies or procedures are when it comes to a diagnosis like this—I will have to check with my manger about it,' that would have showed Paul that Beth was being upfront about any action she was taking, rather than doing it behind his back. Even better would have been for Beth to suggest they go to her manager together, so Paul could hear everything that was being said. It needn't have been such a big deal. Needless to say, one of the first things we did was bring Paul and Beth together to start to have an open conversation about what had been happening.

In order to build trust effectively, we must introduce radical transparency into the way we, as leaders, communicate with our teams. This isn't just a nice idea, but a complete commitment to doing things differently. When you have a culture that demonstrates trust and transparency, rather than secrecy, you no longer have to ask, 'Have they really got a mental illness?' Instead, the question becomes: 'How do we, as a team, help people be even happier and healthier at work?'

Have you ever walked away with the feeling that someone was taking advantage of you in this area? It's possible. If this has ever happened to you, this is a good indication that the toxic fume of distrust has crept into your team

How do you apply this pillar?

At the individual level, when a person has a mental health problem, they often feel completely out of control. This pillar is about giving back some control, so the person feels more empowered and involved. Managers can apply this pillar by simply making a commitment to include the person in any conversations about their mental health and wellbeing or their career.

At the organisational level, it is about making sure there is true engagement of stakeholders at all levels of decision-making about mental health. For example, this could mean including people with an experience of mental ill health in the design of workplace mental health policies, and seeking their input when it comes to planning, implementing and reviewing activities related to mental health and wellbeing. It could also mean gathering feedback about the potential consequences of major workplace changes that are being considered.

Remember, if we are recognising and appreciating the strengths of people with mental health problems, it's a good idea to actively listen to their thoughts on how a planned activity might come across, and what might be useful for them. They will likely have spent much time thinking about these things, so will bring a unique perspective that will be very relevant in this area.

Initiatives

The following is a list of initiatives you could implement to support this pillar:

- Develop policy around transparency and communication and ensure it's acted upon. This means a firm commitment to including the person in conversations about their wellbeing and their job.

- Ensure managers and employees know the requirements with regard to privacy. A person with a mental health issue has certain rights to privacy that must be respected. There are some exemptions when there are safety concerns, so managers need to have a thorough understanding of this.

- Provide training to managers on how to have an open conversation about an employee's mental health and wellbeing with the employee. They don't need to become a counsellor, and their aim is not to fix the situation. But they do need to be able to respond appropriately to someone who discloses mental distress or whom they are concerned about. Managers need to know what they should and shouldn't say.

- Provide transition coaching and support employees leaving the organisation if things aren't working out. It is against the law to fire someone on the basis of a disability, however, it may be that as a result of the person's condition, they simply are not able to perform the inherent requirements of the job. In these cases, businesses are not required to hold the job open for the person. It might be in the best interest of the person and the business that the individual move onto something more suited to their skills and strengths. Where possible, an organisation can make that transition as smooth as possible by providing transition coaching to help that employee move into a new position or company. Transition coaching can involve helping the person to discover what work would be most suited to them, and to move through the process of leaving one workplace and pursuing another path.

- Provide a Managers' Helpline, which specifically assists them to navigate the challenges of managing mental health issues within the workplace. By taking their questions to an independent external provider, who specialises in workplace mental health, managers can maintain privacy and confidentiality, while becoming more educated about this topic and getting answers relevant to the specific situations they face.

- Ensure that the Occupational Health & Safety Committee includes representatives who have an experience of mental ill-health and invite suggestions, comments or feedback in relation to psychological safety as well as physical safety.

Pillar 4

Total Integration

Mentally wealthy organisations see resilience and wellbeing as an integral part of their culture, not just an add-on. To have a mentally healthy workplace, an organisation can't simply bolt on some mental health policies, procedures or activities. It needs to integrate these into existing processes.

Think back to your time in organisations over the past ten to twenty years or so. How many 'strategic initiatives' can you recall? I can think of a stack of them: Total Quality Management, Six Sigma, Employee Onboarding, Activity Based Costing, Management by Objectives, Triple Bottom Line Accounting... and quite a few more. How many of these really stuck and became part of the fabric of the organisation? How many are you actively practising today? Not many, I'd wager.

This is the problem with bolt-on initiatives. The board or the leadership team will get hold of an idea from somewhere and decide it's going to be the next silver bullet to give them a strategic advantage over competitors and transform the industry landscape. Project teams are established, consultants are hired, strategic plans are announced, budgets are approved and work begins. But before long, the project team encounters the headwinds of organisational inertia. When push comes to shove, when a leader's bonus rides on hitting a sales target, for example, they will prioritise business as usual over supporting the project team. With bolt-on initiatives, what looks like commitment is actually in-principle support, as long as it doesn't get in the way of 'the important stuff'.

There is a direct correlation between the mental health of your employees and your organisation's financial performance. It's a no-brainer. Therefore, it is too important to chance employee mental health to the success of your 'Wellness Program' or 'RUOK Awareness Day'. Mental health cannot be an add-on to what you do. It needs to be in built into everything you do. This needs to be a real and authentic assimilation.

When mental health is treated as an add-on, you can get a situation where a mental health policy directly contradicts other policies. For example, the 'wellbeing policy' says we really care, and we are committed to ensuring safe working environments for all, and yet when it comes to the allocation of work, we have one person responsible for a workload which used to be done by three people.

Another situation which arises is the Wellbeing Committee planning a special event or activity (like an annual morning tea for example), where everyone comes together and has their scones, talks about how important mental health is, and that's it for another year. When these events occur in isolation, they are usually seen as being tokenistic, even if that wasn't the intention. If there is already a negative culture within the organisation, this can do way more harm than good.

Immersion

Mental health and wellbeing needs to be part of how you think and how you talk in your organisation. It needs to permeate your policies. It needs to permeate how you move the organisation.

Compare it to physical health and safety. We now understand that everything we do in an organisation has to be done safely. We don't do the 'safety stuff' some of the time and then forget about it for other activities. It is always there. And it needs to be the same with psychological safety.

It can't look like this: 'Oh, did we talk about mental health this quarter? We need to put something in the board report.' No, addressing mental health has to happen as a matter of course.

You can cut logs and carry them to the nearest town and then put them on a truck. Or you can chuck the logs onto the river and let the flow take them to the nearest town. Which one is easier? Don't make your employee mental health initiative a bolt-on that you have to expend additional energy to execute. Make it flow by incorporating it into the way your leaders lead.

Toxic fume: Ignorance

The toxic fume here is ignorance. If people simply aren't aware of mental health and wellbeing as an aspect of everything that happens in the organisation, it just won't work. And efforts to address mental health come across as disingenuous when they're seen as an add-on.

How to apply this pillar

At the individual level, this is about consistency in our interactions with every person. We can't say we care about mental health and that we take it seriously one minute, and then take actions that are not helpful for the person's mental health the next.

At the organisational level, this will mean review of existing policies and processes, not just adding some new ones. It means planning your framework, with ongoing commitment, not just as a one off event.

> **Mentally wealthy organisations see resilience and wellbeing as an integral part of their culture, not just an add-on.**

Initiatives

The following is a list of initiatives you could implement to support this pillar:

- Contract expert consultants to audit workplace mental health and provide recommendations. When we consult with organisations, the first step is to do a stocktake of everything that is in place, and everything that is missing, when it comes to an organisation's wellbeing activities. Then we ask, 'What's working and what's not?' This will usually include a review of policies to ensure they are supportive of mental health and wellbeing and are psychologically safe. We then develop a comprehensive strategy and action plan to put in place. This is more than just a series of activities, and includes targeted changes that are required to really integrate wellbeing into the organisation on a long-term basis.

- Conduct an annual wellbeing survey. This has to be done carefully. There is a way to do this which minimises the risk of harm to the respondents, and avoids creating problems where there are disgruntled employees.

- Call for nominations for a Workplace Wellbeing Coordinator role. When implementing these strategies, it helps to have a dedicated person who is genuinely interested in making a difference in their workplace. That person needn't do everything on their own. In fact, they should get engagement from other employees too, but that one person will coordinate everything and drive the project forward.

- Establish a Mental Health and Wellbeing Committee. This committee will work under the lead of the Workplace Wellbeing Coordinator, and help to communicate and spread any initiatives to across the organisation.

- Pay attention to the physical environment. Paint the walls with colour. Make sure there is sunlight, open spaces with cosy nooks, and dedicated areas for time outs.

- Physical and mental health go hand in hand. Make healthy foods available (e.g. fruit bowls) and access to nutritionists, chiropractors, and other physical health providers. Offer ongoing yoga, gym, meditation and fitness clubs or sports competitions.

- Start a social club, hold a family picnic day and celebrate special events. We know that mental illness and loneliness go together. We are social beings, after all (even the introverts), and we all need to connect from time to time.

Pillar 5

Mutual Responsibility

Mutual responsibility is about moving from a culture of blame—'Who was at fault for what?'—to one of mutual concern, where everyone is seeking a positive outcome.

From a workplace safety perspective, if someone sees a cord in the office over which someone could trip, whose responsibility is it to do something about it?

- The person who left the cord there? Of course, but what if they didn't realise it was unsafe?
- Is it the workplace safety manager? Sure, she's responsible for making the organisation safer, but she's working interstate for the week and knows nothing about the cord.

- Is it the cord-leaving employee's manager? He's accountable for the performance of his employees, but he's been in meetings all morning and hasn't spotted the cord either.

The answer is, of course, *the person who saw the cord.*

Hopefully, you've twigged the metaphor. Everyone shares responsibility for mental health—their own and their team members'.

We must move from a culture of blame:

- 'The employee should have looked after their own health so they could present fit for work.'
- 'The team should have looked after its own a lot better.'
- 'The manager could have avoided this by not being such a slave driver.'
- 'The organisation doesn't provide a physically and psychologically safe workplace.'

…to one of shared concern: *'Yes, all of those statements are true, but it's no one person's responsibility. We're human beings in the same place at the same time, and if someone is unwell, let's take care of each other.'*

Toxic fume: Passing the buck

The toxic fume here is 'passing the buck'. This means blaming anyone or everyone else for the problem.

Let's look at who usually gets blamed:

Blaming the unwell

There are still some managers who say, 'It's not my problem—people should leave their personal issues at home. When you're at work, you're here to work.' Well, that's simply not going to happen. People are people, not robots. It can be very difficult for people to simply 'switch off whatever else is going on for them outside of work. Especially if what is going on means they haven't had a proper night's sleep, or are having a fight or flight response, or suffering from confusion. As a manager, blaming the unwell person isn't going to change the fact that the person is unwell and they are here in front of you in the workplace.

And, besides, who's to say that the issue originated at home? We all know that workplaces themselves can be toxic. And, oftentimes, no amount of self care or emotional intelligence on the part of the unwell person is going to make a difference if the environment they come to everyday is full of bullies, unrealistic expectations or constantly shifting goalposts.

Blaming the manager

Similarly, there are plenty of staff who will always blame the manager. 'If only my manager was more supportive/less directive/different somehow, then I wouldn't be feeling like this! It's their fault I am feeling anxious/depressed/stressed.'

This is the ultimate in personal disempowerment and lack of responsibility. We really don't recommend adopting this 'blame the manager' stance. It is not up to your manager to make you (and everyone else) happy. It's just not going to happen. No one else can 'make' you happy. Sometimes, we do get a bad manager. Maybe they're not a nice person, but more often than not, they are just a person doing their best to juggle competing demands, figure out how to lead a team and hold it all together. Even in those cases where they are at fault, are you really going to give up your happiness and wellbeing because someone else isn't behaving as you think they should? Remember Pillar 1. The person with a mental health problem is not a victim. They have a responsibility for their own life too.

Usually, where someone is blaming the manager, and failing to take responsibility for themselves, organisations will move the person to another department, under another individual. This isn't a bad idea, because, often, too much has happened to be able to repair the relationship. But if nothing is done to change the way the individual interacts with their superior, it won't be long before they are having problems with the next manager too. This is why, alongside addressing mental health problems, all organisations can benefit from building the 'resilience' of their employees. A huge part of building resilience is about a shift in attitude towards taking personal responsibility.

It's not all on the manager's shoulders, and they shouldn't feel the need to move heaven and earth for someone with a mental health issue. Likewise, the person with a mental health issue is not a victim. They're not powerless. They are also responsible for their side of the deal.

Blaming 'management'

And then we have the elusive 'management'. Management usually gets blamed when the unwell individual wants to preserve a relationship with their direct superior, but they still don't want to take responsibility themselves. In these cases, you will hear, 'I know it's not your fault; you're just doing what management says…. But they don't understand what it's really like for us/me.' Or 'Management has a responsibility to provide us with x, y, z for our wellbeing, and they haven't done that.'

Yes, it is true, organisations do have a responsibility to ensure they are providing psychologically safe working environments. But that doesn't make them responsible for the mental wellbeing of every staff member who works there. There are way too many factors involved in a person's wellbeing—the majority of which reside within the individual.

Getting the balance right

Organisations (and industries) tend to be on one side or the other: blaming the individual with an approach that's too tough—'Take a spoonful of cement and toughen up,'—OR blaming management and being too 'touchy feely, anything goes' with the individual. This also doesn't help.

At the end of the day, a person is hired to produce certain outcomes. We shouldn't expect people to produce perfectly 100 per cent of the time, but there also has to be a standard. Lowering the standard does not help a person in distress. It just confirms to them that they are not able to do the job. Instead, what we need to be doing is supporting people to achieve the required outcomes.

Getting the balance right means that all parties, the unwell person, the manager and the organisation, all do what they can within their sphere of control to look after themselves and each other. Taking mutual responsibility means embracing a mature, balanced way of thinking. And it empowers everybody.

Applying this pillar
This pillar empowers individuals (people with mental disorders and their managers) to take action. At the individual level, it's about supporting the person to do what they need to do to stay well. For organisations, it's about taking responsibility for their legal and moral requirements.

Initiatives
The following is a list of initiatives you could implement to support this pillar:

- Seek a statement of commitment to a mentally healthy workplace from your CEO and make sure it's reinforced by action.
- Ensure progress towards a mentally healthy workplace is communicated regularly to all employees.
- Make sure all managers know what their responsibilities are for managing workplace mental health. Make sure they have the skills to do this effectively.

- Regularly remind staff why they were hired. It can be as simple as saying, 'John, I am so pleased to have you on the team. One of the things that stood out to me when I hired you was how you are able think creatively to solve complex problems.' This helps to build personal responsibility with team members.
- End team meetings with shared 'proud and thankfuls'. This involves each person stating something they are proud of, and thanking one person for something they contributed in the week or month.
- Include self-care check-ins in team meetings. This one depends on the culture of the industry and the team. We have observed many teams in health care environments who make it part of their regular meetings to each check in. For example, 'This has been a tough month for me with the loss of x patient or the big project I've been working on. But I'm doing okay.' This allows other people to offer emotional support and also raises awareness of everyone's wellbeing, making it okay to talk about it. But it won't work for every culture. You have to take the temperature of the team before trying to implement something like this.
- Provide training in self-care strategies to build resilience in all staff. It has to be positioned carefully, so it does not look like management is passing the buck to the employees, but done well, this kind of training allows an outsider to come in and encourage staff to take personal responsibility for their own wellbeing, while providing the tools and strategies to do so.
- Ensure self-care strategies are promoted on your intranet, alongside information on mental health and wellbeing, and resources for seeking help should people require it.

Pillar 6

Understanding Complexity

T his pillar recognises that we need to move from very simplistic understandings of mental health to really appreciating the complexity of the topic.

As I'm sure you're beginning to appreciate, mental health is NOT a black and white subject. Human beings are complex, and mental health gets right to the core of human nature. It is not as simple as saying, 'It's a physical condition and we should treat it like one.' After all, it's mental, not physical! And it needs to be treated differently. It's not as simple as saying, 'Go to EAP, or take your meds, and it'll all be okay.' You've seen that that simply doesn't work.

Psychologists spend years in full-time training, and even then only skim the surface of understanding mental health conditions. Remember, even the psychologists and other professionals don't agree on what a mental illness is, let alone what is happening in a specific workplace situation and what should be done to address it. So it's really not a fair expectation to put on a manager to be able to handle these complex situations completely independently. They should definitely get training and continuously upskill themselves, but that will never compare to the expertise of someone who works in this field day in and day out. And nor should it—the role of the manager is to be a manager!

The focus has to be on work. We just need to provide that expert advice and guidance when it's required. The consequences of 'winging it' are just too dire.

Informed actions

We are starting to see organisations respond to the mental health challenges in our workplaces. That's great, as it was previously something that wasn't even on the agenda. You can see it in initiatives designed to build awareness, like 'R U OK? Day.'

Building awareness is a good first step, but the problem comes when you ask someone, 'Are you okay?' and the answer is 'No'. Awareness is powerful, but without knowing what to do next, it's next to useless.

Sometimes, a committee will get together and nut out a whole plan for how they will improve workplace mental health and wellbeing. It is worthwhile having a consultant look over this plan, as they can give you insights into which parts might be the most important, and also which parts might have unintended impacts that the committee hasn't considered. Better yet, have them come in and assess your organisation specifically, so a plan can be created for you.

Toxic fume: Complacency

The toxic fume is complacency—when we think we know enough about something ourselves, rather than seeking expert advice. Even if you've been through a mental health issue yourself, or have supported a family member or friend with one, it doesn't mean you have the full picture when it comes to all the potential issues, especially as they relate to the workplace. Sometimes, a little knowledge can be a dangerous thing!

One of the worst things we have seen workplaces do is nominate someone to attend a mental health course, and then have them come back and deliver that same content internally, as if the material were simply hard, factual information, or they were teaching others how to operate a piece of equipment. This is a recipe for disaster. That person will not have the in-depth understanding of the material to be able to deliver it in a way that empowers people, in a way that gently affects a shift in attitude where required. They will definitely not be able to answer questions that go beyond the scope of the specific materials. And they will not have the training to be able to observe the audience and support the participants through what many consider to be very sensitive subject matter.

Even if the person has some background or interest in psychology, if their role is to be a manager, they're not going to be in the position of being a mental health educator day in and day out—someone who knows what's needed to get the best result for your people. Not to mention, people always tend to listen more openly to an expert from outside the organisation as opposed to a colleague or manager.

This kind of decision demonstrates, at best, a lack of understanding of the complexity of mental health, and, at worst, complacency.

The right approach

I've often reflected on the role of the manager being 'to bring certainty and structure to unstructured situations.' When things don't go to plan, managers like to have a process for figuring out what's wrong and how to fix it. Unfortunately, people are incredibly complex. They have different goals and values. Different work styles and preferences. Different belief structures. And events affect them differently. There is no manual for fixing a mental health problem—only a range of approaches you can try, some of which seem to work better than others.

The point we're making is that, for a manager, there isn't much to be gained by being able to diagnose a mental illness and prescribe a treatment plan. It's not your job to do so. But by recognising that people and situations are complex, taking a step back, and coming at the problem with an enquiring mind, and an intention to help the individual, you can achieve a lot.

Applying this pillar

Be discerning when it comes to what you listen to. There is no consensus around mental health. When you look globally, the professionals and institutions who are getting better results do not work with the traditional top-down approaches. In many cases, we see these traditional, medical 'one size fits all' responses making things worse. Suicide is increasing, not decreasing, despite more 'awareness', for example. People are being educated to be unwell, not self-empowered. Instead, look for education that is 'recovery-oriented'. It's not a guarantee, but it's more likely that it will contain information based on the latest evidence base.

At the individual level, we can apply this pillar by recognising the unique circumstances and explanations of each person, and not trying to 'solve' the mental health issue for the employee. Know the limits of your role and expertise and don't be afraid to ask for help if you need it.

For the organisation, it is about seeking expert advice in the planning and delivery of workplace mental health activities, so they really do get the desired outcomes for the business and the employees, rather than simply ticking boxes and making everyone feel good that they've done something.

Initiatives

The following is a list of initiatives you could implement to support this pillar:

- Provide refresher mental health training on a regular basis. We recommend including a module on mental health as part of induction, and that training be held at least every year or two, depending on the size of the organisation. This helps to keep it forefront in people's minds.

- Provide specialist training for supervisors about managing mental health issues and creating a mentally healthy work culture. Managers need more than the basics. They need to know their legal responsibilities and how to manage the intricacies of mental health appropriately.

- Offer online learning opportunities in mental health. Online training is a great way to teach a large number of staff in dispersed locations about mental health, in bite-sized chunks of time.

- Train leaders in advanced supervision skills. Encourage leaders to have regular 'supervision' meetings with their employees. Usually, once a month works well. This time allows both the manager and the employee to check in, ask, 'Are we okay?' and raise any issues or concerns they might be having. This can pre-empt a lot of problems before they become too big to handle.

- Create a leadership induction program for all new managers / supervisors. Being able to manage mental health issues effectively relies largely on having good leadership, management and communication skills. When managers have a strong foundation of leadership skills, they will be able to implement mental health specific actions much more effectively.

- Provide training to managers in sound performance management processes. It is very common for mental health issues to rise to the surface when in the midst of a performance management process. Managers need to know how to handle each thing independently, and also what to do when the two issues become combined.

Pillar 7

Wrap-around Strategies

I n this pillar, we are moving away from Band-Aid solutions to mental wealth initiatives. We need to move beyond ticking boxes. We need to look for actions which will really get results and make a difference for our organisations and the people in them. A preference for integrating mental health initiatives over applying Band-Aid solutions demonstrates an organisation's commitment to 'wrap-around strategies'.

Too often, organisations tend to focus narrowly on only one aspect of mental health.

Typically, it is either to focus on 'building awareness' or on 'first responders'. Both are very good initiatives to have in place, but they are only small pieces of the puzzle.

Awareness programs are useful, but they can't be the only strategy. One example of an awareness program used in isolation would be to put up some posters on wellbeing, perhaps leave a few flyers around the place, and that's it. Sure, you might get a couple of people who notice the poster, but does it change anything about the way in which people interact with each other? Or does it send the message that you shouldn't feel sad or anxious, and if you do—go get help somewhere else? Of course, that's not the intention, but that's what can happen. Also, beware of posters that make people start to feel worse. We've seen some that list a whole range of symptoms—Do you feel a, b, c, d and so on...? And does it feel really awful?' By the time you've finished reading, you're starting to feel all those things! And going into a panic. Not helpful.

Many organisations decide to train some people as 'first responders'. Again, this is a very good idea. There should be people who know how to respond to someone who is becoming unwell or in a mental health emergency. Unfortunately, this is often done as a reactive measure, after an incident has occurred where the workplace realised they didn't know what to do. Better late than never, but it would have been much better to do this before anything happened. Especially in the case of suicide. The other part that is often forgotten is how the program is communicated to the organisation at large. Does anyone even know that there are first responders around whom they can speak to if they want to? Do the first responders get any follow up support, or is it a matter of: 'We had twenty people attend the training so they're all good to go now. We don't need to speak of this again. We've done our bit'? What happens if they get busy with other things?

Some organisations don't even go that far. They might have an Employee Assistance Program in place, and that's it. We're sorry to tell you that most people won't access that EAP program, and if they do, they may or may not go back to it. Typically, these programs have a very poor uptake, for a huge range of reasons. You can't rely on an EAP service to get the outcomes you are looking for.

Toxic fume: Being reactive

The toxic fume here is being reactive. We don't want a situation where there needs to be a crisis before we put some plans or activities in place. We need a combination of prevention, early intervention, and elegant response systems.

You know the saying: Prevention is better than cure. Those who do apply this in workplaces get better results.

Elements of your strategy

We need to think more broadly than the bookend strategies of making people aware of the potential for trouble and mopping up after it happens.

Prevention

You need to look at your prevention strategies. What do you have in place to minimise and prevent mental health problems from developing or escalating within your workplace? Obviously, people will go through the various challenges that life brings, but if work can be a safe place, that can play a huge part in providing stability.

Prevention strategies can include activities targeted at building resilience within the workforce. Remember the 'commando' analogy. Wouldn't it be great to have a team of people who can show up, completely committed to getting the job done, with a 'no excuses' attitude, and ready to overcome any hurdle thrown at them?

This can also include more general wellness programs. The link between physical and mental health is well established, so what do you offer in the way of gym memberships, walking groups, walking desks, private health care, and so on?

Leadership development programs fall under this category. When managers are trained to be effective leaders, they can better create an environment and a culture where people are happy to come to work every day.

Early intervention

You need to look at your early intervention strategies. These are the processes and procedures you have in place to respond when someone might be beginning to become unwell. It includes teaching your workforce what the warning signs of mental ill-health are, and how to recognise these in yourself or others, as well as what to do in the cases where you do see some signs. How do you react without overreacting?

What information is there available for people to get help from a range of sources, according to their filter? Do you have an intranet with a wellbeing section?

Crisis response

Unfortunately, despite your best efforts, some people will become unwell through no fault of their own or anyone else's. We can do lots to prevent it, but at the end of the day, that's life, and it throws curveballs. Do your people know what to do if someone has a panic attack? If someone says that they are thinking about suicide? If someone has a psychotic episode on site?

What about your Return To Work procedures? Do your managers know how to manage that appropriately? Is it working? Sometimes, we might have been given advice on what is required, for example, if the person needs medical clearance to return to work. The person may provide it, but they are still behaving in ways which are of concern to management. Do your leaders know what to do then? Do they have the procedures to follow and the training to know how to implement them?

Do you have all these angles addressed? As you can see, each of these initiatives by themselves is useful, but when used in isolation, they have little sustainable impact. If they do all exist, how are they working? Are people engaging fully? Are they being utilised?

....

A preference for considered mental health initiatives over Band-Aid solutions demonstrates an organisation's commitment to wrap-around strategies

....

How do you apply this pillar?

Building a mentally wealthy culture doesn't require a massive bolt-on program; it requires you to ensure the psychological needs of a diverse workforce are catered for. Diversity is not just about age, gender or ethnicity, but diversity in working style, talent and life outlook too.

At an individual level, managers need to make sure they have all the stages covered in terms of how they look after all team members' wellbeing in the absence of any problems, how they identify stress early if any team member is struggling, and how they respond for early intervention or in a crisis situation.

At an organisational level, prevention strategies like resilience programs, supportive policies, and management training save a lot of time, money and suffering for everyone. However, even with best prevention strategies, humans will become unwell sometimes. So we do need the others too. We need to know how to identify and respond to people who might be becoming unwell, or who are having a mental health emergency.

Where to start will differ for every organisation, depending on their current climate and priorities. But regardless of your starting point, make sure to develop some targeted wrap-around strategies.

Initiatives

In addition to some of the suggestions laid out above, we also re-commend:

- Developing a comprehensive mental health action plan to guide your activities for the next twelve months. Review this annually and update.
- Reviewing all policies to make sure they are in line with mental health and wellbeing.
- Deciding on the protocols for each stage of mental ill-health. E.g. if you're concerned for someone, if someone discloses mental ill-health, if someone requires emergency care, if someone is absent on mental health leave, if someone is retuning to work, etc. These procedures need to be clear enough that managers know what to do, but not so prescriptive that they don't allow for the individual needs of the person. Policies are there to serve, not to constrain. You will need to seek expert assistance for this.
- Call for nominations for Mental Health First Responders and provide training. We find it better to ask for volunteers than to nominate people. When individuals are nominated, they can sometimes feel entitled to special treatment. It's much better to ask for volunteers who genuinely want to be involved, and then select those best positioned and suited to help.
- Make a Wellness Recovery Action Plan (WRAP) available to all and ensure it's completed as part of induction training. This is similar to completing 'next of kin' details for a physical emergency, but has a few additional questions on what to do in the case of a mental health emergency.

Conclusion

S o, how are you going? That was a lot of information, wasn't it? It is necessary information though. You see, what we've been doing so far hasn't worked. Why?

At the broader level, as a society, we've attempted to reduce what is an intricate and complex human issue, into neat and tidy boxes and checklists. We've put our focus on the individual with the 'problem' instead of looking at the situation holistically, with an understanding of the interactions between individuals and our environments. We've strayed so far from our initial understandings of human nature that lots of words are needed to bring us back to basics.

And specifically, in businesses and organisations, what workplaces have been doing, hasn't t the outcomes they've been looking for. Most companies' default response has been to refer people to Employee Assistance Programs, or sick leave. While there's a role for those two actions, it's not wise that they've become so key in dealing with mental health problems.

Let's face it, it hasn't worked.

Now you know better.

So what will you **do** with this? As a manager you are required to do more than just to be simply 'aware'. You are called to action. To respond. And to respond elegantly, exquisitely, effectively. Of course, that's not just an obligation for you, it's also a privilege and an honour. A service of high calibre to your fellow human beings in distress.

Managers able to hold their own in this space are needed. Leaders that can show both empathy and business focus, at the same time, are the ones making the difference today. Tokenistic approaches are quickly losing their strength. People are becoming smarter and can tell what's fake. Even when delivered with sincerity.

The good news is that, if you've come so far as to have read this book, then you are truly on your way to deliver in a massive and positive way. You know that being able to diagnose or counsel is not required. What is required is that you 1) understand the psychological dynamics that exist in workplaces and 2) prevent problems by creating healthy cultures; and 3) are available to your colleagues in difficult times.

Building a mentally wealthy culture doesn't require a massive bolt on program, but it does require you to ensure the psychological needs of a diverse workforce are catered for. Diverse not just in age, gender or ethnicity, but diversity in work style, talent and life outlook.

As you apply even a few of the principles and techniques explained in this book, you'll discover how fast they work. You'll also see your circle of influence expand for good.

Let the 7 Pillars of a Mentally Wealthy Workplace guide you. They are there to protect you and your team. Come back to this book and revise them often:

1. We not You, we are in this together and if one of us has a problem, we all have a problem
2. Organisational Plasticity—just like your brain, your organisation should be plastic. Make sure you are flexible in how you approach your staff's needs.
3. Nothing About Me Without Me—involve the person from the very start in any and all conversations about them.
4. Total Integration—make wellbeing and mental health deeply ingrained in everything you do and say
5. Mutual Responsibility—don't pass the buck. Mental health is everyone's responsibility
6. Understanding Complexity—keep learning. Keep applying what you learn. There are nuances to this topic that take time to master
7. Wrap Around Strategies—build procedures to tackle the different stages of mental distress and its recovery. If you don't know, consider bringing the experts in.

Remember that a mentally wealthy organisation is well worth the effort now. There are all the good reasons we have explored in this book: more profit, a better culture, more creativity and innovation. It protects you from liability. And then there are the moral benefits of knowing you've done the right thing.

Recognition of mental wealth is a paradigm shift. We realize that. So kudos for you still being here, not throwing the book down and running away. What you have been told about leading successfully: the macho, tough leadership style (even when dressed up with some sophistication and political correctness) creates less valuable companies in the long run than displaying genuine compassion and a willingness to work with people to achieve a common goal.

That's why our approach is such a game changer.

So just one question remains: What will YOU do from here?

Commit to taking one action today that will improve the mental health and wellbeing of your team or organisation.

If you need help, or want to support to make changes, contact our office at admin@wmhi.com.au. We're always there to help. Just reach out. We'd love to hear from you.

To your continued success,

Peter Diaz & Emi Golding

• •

The Employee Wellbeing Survey is designed to highlight where your areas of opportunity are when it comes to the mental health and wellbeing of your workforce It only takes about ten to fifteen minutes to complete and it provides a good overall risk assessment of your organisational culture, leadership, education and policies surrounding mental health as well as recommendations on how to make positive change in your organisation. To conduct the Employee Wellbeing Survey in your organisation, contact us at admin@wmhi.com.au and mention this book.

• •

About the Authors
And the Workplace Mental
Health Institute

Peter Diaz

Peter Diaz is founder and CEO and of the Workplace Mental Health Institute (WMHI). An accredited Mental Health Social Worker by profession, he is also the author of *Reclaim Your Power* and a highly respected international speaker on the topic of workplace mental health, leadership, resilience, emotional intelligence and diversity.

Peter's professional experience includes positions as a psychological injury expert for GIO Insurance, a visiting fellow at the University of Wollongong, a field educator for the Australian Catholic University, and the NSW President of the Australian Association of Social Workers. He has also worked in community mental health services as a senior manager, where he is known for his expertise in change management and the development of recovery-oriented programs and workforces.

Having experienced mental disorder (bipolar disorder) and having fully recovered, Peter understands firsthand the challenges of managing a mental health problem and what is needed for recovery. He's also seen the damage that unattended mental health issues can have not only for the person experiencing them, but also for those around them, including their family, friends and colleagues.

Peter's mission is to revolutionise the way mental health is approached around the world, by providing cutting edge, unique and honest education programs to workplaces that get real results—both for the business and the people in it.

Peter has helped Fortune 500 companies increase profits by enhancing the mental health, wellbeing, resilience and productivity of their workforce. He's helped thousands of people and businesses become empowered, so they can thrive.

He has interviewed business giants like Steve Wozniak (co-founder of Apple), and Randi Zuckerberg (marketing genius behind Facebook) on the topics of employee engagement, workplace wellbeing, and resilience. And he has featured in numerous media publications including BBC, SBS, ABC, Business Insider, Daily Telegraph and Woman's Day.

Emi Golding

Emi Golding is a registered Psychologist, Fortune 500 Consultant, Executive and Business Coach, and Founder of the Workplace Mental Health Institute. A member of the Australian Psychological Society, Emi has many years' experience in the mental health sector, working on the frontline and in senior management positions, as well as with individuals in private practice.

Emi has developed an extensive understanding of the complexities of mental disorders as well as what is needed to overcome them.

Emi was an expert panel member for the development of guidelines for organisations on the prevention of mental disorders in the workplace, and she is particularly passionate about suicide prevention. She regularly provides consultation to organisations on the psychological safety of their workplaces.

An accomplished businesswoman, Emi has also spoken on stages in the USA, Australia, Europe and South Africa, and regularly collaborates with high level business partners around the world.

She is a Master Practitioner of NLP and provides executive and business coaching to senior leaders and business owners internationally, and has been featured in global publications including Woman Entrepreneur and 'Fear to Freedom'.

Workplace Mental Health Institute

Established by Peter Diaz and Emi Golding, the Workplace Mental Health Institute specialises in helping organisations to improve their productivity and profitability by ensuring the psychological safety of their workplaces.

The Workplace Mental Health Institute is the only organisation specialising in workplace wellbeing who offer a complete solution for improving employee engagement, productivity and business results.

The Workplace Mental Health Institute partners with corporate, governments, and community organisations across the world, to assess their specific situation, identify the root cause of any problems, develop an evidence based plan of action, and implement it effectively to get tangible results for the people and the bottom line.

The mission is to strengthen people and organisations from the inside out, by delivering recovery focussed mental health education and consultation that is refreshingly honest, unique and gets results.

Printed in the USA
CPSIA information can be obtained
at www.ICGtesting.com
JSHW082342140824
68134JS00020B/1834

9 781642 793666